Diarmuid Gavin's Big Ideas

to Justine

Diarmuid Gavin's Big Ideas

Contents

Introduction   **6**

Living   **28**
Case study: Eyes Wide Shut   46

Dens   **56**
Case study: Egghead   72

Planting   **82**
Case study: Meteor   108

Levels   **118**
Case study: Box of Tricks   138

Enclosures   **148**
Case study: Elevation   166

Acknowledgements   178
Suppliers   180
Index   188

Introduction

In today's society, more than ever, people are fascinated by gardening. The new breed of gardener that has emerged is a design-aware suburbanite with more disposable income than ever before; couple this with a newly garnered appreciation for his or her surroundings and is it any wonder that in the last decade or so gardening has become the number one leisure activity in Britain?

I would love to see gardening become an interest that is hip and cool for young people, and for it to continue to throw off the slightly academic image that it has acquired over the last fifty years. The media, including television, have embraced gardening as an entertainment as well as a lifestyle option, and through some of these television programmes, people have started to understand and explore the qualities and the potential functions of their plot. But to create a new, younger breed of gardeners from the next generation, we have to grab their attention from the other distractions of modern-day life: we need to create gardens that fascinate, that entertain, that challenge and that have a place in today's hectic lifestyle. It might sound like an impossible task to create something so dramatically new, but new ideas can work hand-in-hand with our more traditional gardening styles and aspirations.

Many more of us than ever before have gardens, and a huge group of us see them as an important part of our homes. Gardens are increasingly valued as a place of refuge, somewhere to relax and take stock (see Enclosures on p.152), but equally, they are becoming places to entertain and an extension of our homes and indoor spaces (see Living on p.31 and Dens on p.58). The needs of the individual have changed and, with increasing wealth and access to a new culture of good design, we have a combination that allows us to translate our fantasies into a practical and aesthetically pleasing reality.

The ingredients that go into creating a garden are very few. The reasons that gardens are created are quite simple. However, the selections that evolve from reasons and ingredients can lead to an intoxicating and newly appreciable array of styles and designs. Throughout history, there have been different motivations for creating gardens – from the spiritual needs of ancient religions to design their mythical gardens, to the more practical and physical need of humankind to build enclosures for containing or growing food.

Garden design in history

In the context of needing to understand and wanting to create our modern gardens, it is important to examine the bequest of history.

In previous centuries, money played a large part in defining the designs for gardens – they were the playthings of the rich to display their wealth and to entertain, with parklands for hunting and large herb and vegetable plots to sustain huge households. On a less material plane were gardens such as the oasis gardens of the desert and the medieval monastery gardens with herbs, fishponds and flowers for the altar, that represented, in many ways, an expression of their creators' vision of paradise.

Some of the earliest recorded gardens were those of the Egyptians. Their gardens were centred on the fruitfulness of the oasis – water was the most important element and became the central motif, both by necessity

and symbolism. This garden style evolved into different forms, but it originally came to Europe with the Moorish invaders of southern Spain. It is a style that has constantly changed as it has been adopted by different cultures and even reinterpreted by different religions – it is, primarily, an Islamic garden style, but the Christian cloister gardens also owe much to its tradition. Today, we still see its impact as a courtyard garden with a central fountain, or as a contemporary design with shallow rills or canals rippling through them.

In Europe, garden design found its own varied style based on a different cultural background. The ancient Greeks and Romans evolved the concept of a garden as a place, not just for the production of food, but to enjoy or to be used for hunting or as a homage to paradise. They incorporated art and architecture in the garden in the form of classical statuary and temples. The Roman gardens were also the precursor of the outdoor room; their gardens were placed – courtyard-style – at the centre of the house.

Moving on a few thousand years, when we think of Italian Renaissance gardens, we see steep terraces carved into a hillside. The essence of this garden style is a composition that is in harmony with the surrounding beauty of the countryside. The aim is not to subjugate nature, but celebrate it and design hand-in-hand with its demands. Terracing was the solution to the hilly landscape and these terraces were flanked by wooded areas to frame the view from the house, define the limits of the terrace and merge the garden into the landscape

beyond. The Renaissance brought with it a renewed appreciation of art and sculpture, and carved stonework and wrought iron found its way into the garden, often decorating these terraces.

Over in England, there was a revolution in styles in the eighteenth century when many formal gardens with their straight lines, parterres, fountains and flowerbeds were destroyed to make way for the new landscape style. Typified by the work of William Kent and Lancelot 'Capability' Brown, their rolling hills, artificial lakes and ruined temples were inspired by Italian landscape paintings. The 'ha-ha' – a ditch instead of fence or hedge – was an important development of this style that served both practical and aesthetic purposes: it keeps cattle out whilst allowing an uninterrupted view, giving the impression that the garden blended seamlessly with the countryside beyond. Much of this design style was based on an exhibition of wealth. Later still, the Industrial Revolution in Britain brought with it a new wealth and prosperity, which landowners poured into their estates. This new money also allowed for travel, both for design inspiration and the sponsorship of Victorian plant hunters to visit far-off countries and send home exotic, unheard-of plants for the great glasshouses and gardens of their wealthy patrons.

The twentieth century brought with it devastating wars and, in the wake of the Second World War, whole areas of towns needed to be rebuilt having been destroyed by the bombing. This, and the increased wealth over the

past decades, created a revolution in style and architecture and in new construction techniques that would slowly filter through into modern garden design. A new glamour broke through from Hollywood too, and the Californian lifestyle became the new aspiration – a lifestyle that was firmly based on outdoor living.

Modern garden design

There has been a bewildering succession of changes in the arts over the past century. All forms of artistic expression have moved on – new generations can feel disenfranchised from their parents' taste and youth itself brings with it a desire for new forms of self-expression. Culture has always carried with it the seeds of change and the culture of today is the influence of tomorrow. Most artistic disciplines have sought continually to reinvent themselves, paying little heed to snobbery, elitism and, in some cases, practicality. But although innovation, experimentation and risk-taking continued to be key across horticulture in general, the art of garden design remained relatively stilted.

Modern architecture has proved it can be fun and irreverent as well as functional and beautiful; it has brought a new vision and excitement to design that we can all benefit from and should not be afraid to be influenced by. The new architecture brought with it a wide range of materials that were so carefully developed that they can now also find a place in domestic, small-scale situations – and as we have brought them into our

homes, why not bring them into our gardens too? (See p.60).

And yet, gardens still seem to evolve only slowly. What we have learnt about gardening through the millennia is precious – the styles that have been handed down to us from all ages and all parts of the world are still important, and are overwhelmingly valid today. In modern garden design, we don't have to slavishly copy or reinvent an existing genre, but we can look to these examples and incorporate elements of them into our own designs. We can develop designs for a modern-day setting – learning from the lessons of what came before, but experimenting with the ideas for our own time so that we can leave inspiration for the next generation of gardeners and designers. In order to do this, we must examine what gardens or outdoor space mean to us now and define our needs and aspirations.

In the 1920s, '30s and '40s, architects and designers took their ideas outside and, to a degree, developed the contemporary idea of the 'room outdoors'. It has become a much-used phrase, but it is still the best way to describe the revolution that has allowed non-gardeners to become gardeners, without being able to reel off a load of Latin plant names. Many of us feel comfortable with decorating our homes and know exactly what we need in and from them, but for most of us, gardening has long instilled a slight feeling of panic and the fear of not being able to translate this design confidence outdoors.

So what have we learnt from history and the recent past in garden design, and what is regarded as progressive and new in the garden today? Late in the twentieth century and at the beginning of the twenty-first century, a new and interesting debate has emerged: what makes a garden and what is an installation? The very ideas of what we should accept in our private and public spaces outdoors are being turned on their heads.

We have been so bound up in the traditional ideas of creating, using and maintaining gardens that it may be necessary to forget everything we know and start afresh. To truly regard the garden as a blank canvas – an open space to be developed in any way we choose – could be a liberating and enlightening thing. But those who grasp this seductive principle will often be subjected to the restrictive views of outsiders. In conservative societies, the cry can often be about what the neighbours will say and the dread of ridicule by family members or friends for trying something new. If it is your garden and you want to create a garden that expresses some excitement and a forward way of thinking, you'll have to be brave. It takes an adventurous spirit and the courage of convictions, as in every area of artistic expression. But it always takes one person to buck the trend first.

So let's start off with irreverence: we will not dismiss everything we know, but we will, at least, try to let down our guard a bit.

Garden design in the future

The boundaries of garden design have opened up in recent years, and designers and homeowners alike are being much more experimental with their landscaping and choice of plants. As the next generation grows up feeling more at ease with, and with a better understanding of gardens and garden design, we can expect a fascinating future.

In so many areas of our lives, the conveniences of technology have made busy lifestyles much easier and more enjoyable. Low-maintenance gardens have become much more desirable and even lighting and electrical points have sneaked into the garden. But there are so many more unexplored possibilities: gardens could be mobilized – borders filled with plants could travel on wheels or tracks, or the patio could move around the garden following the sun. Your lawn could be transformed into a magical carpet by night with twinkling, white, fibre-optic lights rippling through it, which will still be safe for the mower the following morning. Movies outdoors will become commonplace as high-definition projectors become cheaper. New awnings, not ugly canopies, will be developed, so that we can be sure of favoured conditions when hosting a party, and new ranges of furniture in weather-resistant fabrics will be in the shops to suit any taste. Under-floor heating will move outside and make a cold stone floor warm to bare feet. You'll be able to choose from a selection of microclimates just for your plot that will be automatically controlled to take account of natural conditions. Plants

will be bought as large specimens; indeed whole, fully developed borders will be available for your appreciation.

OK, so a lot of this might seem like fantasy right now, but all this is possible in the not-too-distant future. Until then, of course, some of these ideas can be used as inspiration for what you can achieve already in your garden.

Inspiration

Inspiration plays a major role in design – it motivates and stimulates, but above all, it is intensely personal. True inspiration is about what moves the individual – and you may not even know why it affects you. In our society, we are surrounded by images from advertising, the media, fashion and design from our own country and abroad. Often, travelling to other countries can bring a sense of freedom and the experience of a new culture and we will want to bring these sensations home with us. This has brought many different styles into our homes and gardens. We can echo or completely imitate Mediterranean or Japanese gardens, or more exotic, tropical styles. In the horticultural world, this global influence has been present for decades – from the Victorian plant hunters bringing back new and unseen species, through the impact of conifers and heathers in the '60s, to our current fascination with growing exotics outside in our gardens that once were confined to the great glasshouses of the rich.

When people ask me where my inspiration comes from, I can only say 'from everywhere'. It arrives from the constant observation of shape, form, colour and effect. It may be looking at a pair of sunglasses and wondering why a lawn has never been shaped and contoured along the same lines. When something like that happens, there's a real sense of excitement. It's not a sense of 'Oh great, there's another garden', or 'There's another idea for another structure'; it's more like 'Why haven't I seen that done before? Why haven't I done it before? What would it be like?' My real inspiration comes from experience, rather than from years of education and the knowledge of traditional horticulture that I gleaned from them.

And for me, inspiration also comes from knowing which materials I love or hate. For example, I think the potential of metal is great, but to understand what you can do with different types of metal in its many forms, you have to understand their particular qualities. And learning about a material's qualities, learning about its strengths and weaknesses, often leads to a sense of what can be done with it. Sometimes, when I'm really beginning to understand the makeup of a material, it sparks off ideas that seem to transcend its possibilities.

Technology and entertainment is full of excitement and yet I am amazed that we rarely bring it outdoors, either to use it in a 'normal' way, such as showing a movie or piping sound out from a CD player, or to use it in a subversive, surreal way. The flickering images from

television have always appealed to me – the way colours and light levels are constantly changing but with a very luminous quality. I love the idea of television sets – or even computer monitors – being set into the ground as paving slabs to form a pathway. Or even set into a lawn or beneath planting. That idea had one of its origins in Michael Jackson' 'Billie Jean' video, in which he danced down a studio set made up to look like a New York street scene. As his feet touched each paving slab, they illuminated like magic. That led me to dream up ideas of paving slabs in gardens lighting either when touched or just to give a constantly changing visual effect.

Sometimes the inspiration for an idea or a complete garden is not at all obvious, and it's only later that you recognize where the spark could have come from or how you involuntarily may have interpreted something you had seen in the past. So it's a type of subliminal effect – walking around the South Beach area of Miami or even appreciating the deco-inspired look of much of London Underground architecture, helped the evolution of a garden in Ealing, north London. The ideas behind what you see and the reasons for the style being used in their various forms stay in your head and eventually may come out when the location requirements and the client match. Or it may be that you just continually marvel at technology, how exciting it is that hydraulics and mechanics and car engineering could possibly be reworked to make a whole garden move (see Elevation on p.166). It may be the physical beauty of the female

form can be reinterpreted in the sensuous curves and warm wood of a garden enclosure (see Curvy on p.158).

Planting inspiration is very different and extremely personal. Of course it can be and will often be inspired by the particular site and situation you're in, taking regard of climatic conditions and likes and dislikes of the garden owner. But for me it's not so much about physical travel, it's about a different journey, a personal understanding of what plants mean to you and how best you can interpret them on their own or in groups in different schemes. My relationship with plants and the way I use them continues to evolve. In recent times, because of an appreciation of climate change and global ecological concerns, the pendulum for me is swinging back from the more dramatic introductions (trendy since the 1990s), to a more equal use of native plants, old-fashioned herbaceous perennials and tolerant exotics. The understanding that often dramatic architectural forms created using structures in gardens can be toned down and blended in to a landscape site using softer species has been a continuing theme in my outlook on an overall garden. The grander the scheme, the more gentle the planting, seems to be a new rule.

Planning your garden

So, you've had a good look around and seen different styles of landscaping, planting and materials and you know exactly the sort of garden you are going to go for. What next? Well, there are some rules and regulations to

take into account. The most important thing to remember is that a garden will not work unless it exists in a practical and functional way – if a garden doesn't meet your needs, it doesn't work. The gardens I create for television have a requirement to initiate debate, to move things on and to try something new on a weekly basis. This can be quite difficult but great fun, but it is, however, best to see what we do on *Home Front in the Garden* as a deviation from the norm.

Your requirements

If we progress logically through the steps, you will see that it is relatively easy to come up with a scheme that fulfils your requirements. Firstly, you should clarify your personal likes and dislikes, because these can sometimes get lost in a scenario where there seems to be an overwhelming choice of style and content. When deciding on what you need, remember to listen to everything that is being said by everyone in your household. Gardens can be made to be successful and enjoyable for all members of the family, and that's what all members of the family will expect too! Don't end up with a situation where mum and dad are overjoyed with the pristine creation, but where the children have no place for swings, slides or to play football; at worst, they'll destroy your beautiful garden in an attempt to find a play space.

Consider, too, who is going to look after the garden and when? Are you a keen gardener, or does deadheading and weeding fill you with boredom?

Is gardening a hobby or a chore? A proper garden will develop over time, so you need to establish the boundaries of maintenance and how you expect the garden to perform over the years. If you do decide you want a garden with all the joys of pruning and mowing, it is a good idea to have rear access – unless you don't mind carrying bags of garden rubbish through the house. Equally, this should feature in your initial plans when deciding if you need a skip to clear out the existing garden before you lay down the new one.

Before you start writing lists of plants or start laying a patio, take a look at your garden as it is currently laid out. Roughly sketch your plot and then get out a tape measure and take down some measurements. You will need to take into account any fixed features that will be staying, and any existing planting that you would like to salvage. Be sensible, though, decide which plants are doing well and which aren't and don't hang onto the straggling specimens in the hope that they might perk up. At this point, dig a hole to see what the groundwork and the soil are like and then conduct a very simple pH test. It's not as scientific and confusing as it sounds. The kits from garden centres are easy to use, and could explain why your acid-loving rhododendrons look so sad, and why it's not worth planting them again.

Style and substance

Once you've decided on the practical elements of your garden, start to think about the style. If you haven't

already decided on the exact style for your design, spend some time thinking about what you like in terms of mood, materials, colour and texture. A tear sheet sequence can be extremely useful in trying to establish your likes and dislikes; I find it the most enlightening way of discovering what a client wants. There's no trick to it: simply go through magazines and books and cut and paste together the styles and items that you really like on one sheet, and those you strongly dislike on another.

When deciding on your hard landscaping, consider the qualities of one material over another – there is a wide range of decking available now, including hard- and softwoods, grooved decking, and a vast array of sizes and colours of tiles, slabs and stone. If you can get hold of some samples, live with them for a while and debate their merits until you find the right material for your purposes. Before you lay down any hard landscaping, think about whether or not you want to include any water or electric cables – there are loads of entertainment features, such as lighting, sound systems and projector screens, that you can incorporate into your design if the means of powering them is thought about initially.

Which leads us onto one very important consideration: budget. Be aware of the costs involved in what you plan to do, and be realistic about what you are prepared to spend – it's always disappointing to have to scale back your plans once underway because you have run out of funds. At the same time, be prepared to spend a bit more than you might on redecorating your sitting room – it may seem a

lot of expense, but bear in mind that a well-designed garden should outlast fashion and will not need to be redone every few years – if anything, it should look better with age. On *Home Front in the Garden*, we often bring in mature planting so that we can show the finished effect of the garden without waiting for it to mature. Obviously such plants are expensive, so you might have to buy younger plants and be patient while your garden grows.

Legal constraints

If you are planning to construct any buildings in your garden, bear in mind that some changes that are made to your garden may need approval from the local authority. What you can and can't do without permission depends on where you live and what you're planning to do. It may be that you are completely free to carry on at your will, or you might have to submit detailed plans and proposals, not only for new structures but for any physical changes you intend to make to buildings or indeed plants. There are no hard and fast rules here; the requirements vary enormously and it is always best before you start any work to contact your local authority building officer, explain what you intend to do and see what the rules and regulations are. This is especially important if you live in a conservation area or listed property, as the requirements there are strict and specific, and in most urban or suburban areas there are even rules that limit the pruning or removal of trees. Remember that your local authority can make you take down anything that doesn't comply with regulations.

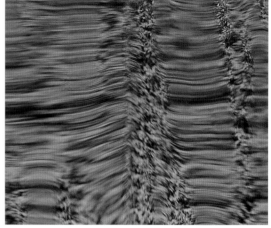

Most local authorities will mainly be concerned with assessing the height of boundary walls or fences and the height and material construction of any structures within the garden. A safe rule to work by is that in an unrestricted area, boundary walls can be built to a height of 2m (6½ft) and external structures can be 3m (10ft) tall, as long as they are at least 1m (3ft) from each boundary wall. If you want to build a wall next to a road, you may be limited by highway regulations to 1m (3ft) unless you get special permission. Wooden buildings, such as sheds, are acceptable in most cases without planning permission as they are viewed as temporary structures.

One final piece of advice when planning your garden: it is good policy, as well as good manners, to alert your neighbours to any garden construction you decide to undertake. Do remember that any work you do might affect their view from their home or garden as well as their access to light and could cause problems between you. If they feel they have been part of a consultative process and that you have listened and taken account of their concerns, you may avoid protracted and uncomfortable situations afterwards.

And so now is the time to read through the rest of this book. The next few chapters will show a variety of different approaches to various design ideas: your living spaces, dens, how to create levels and private spaces, planting styles, and a few quirky ideas to prove that your garden can be about whatever you want it to be.

Golden rules for designing your garden

- Examine your requirements and desires very carefully before you put pen to paper.
- Decide on the essence and style of the new garden to be created.
- Examine and come to know your site.
- Carefully measure up the site and include all features, whether plants or structures, on your site survey.
- Consider whether there are any features that need to be disguised, such as garages, oil tanks, maintenance areas or sheds.
- Consider what functional things need to be in the garden to make it work, such as a waste disposal area, clothesline, greenhouse, or incinerator.
- Develop your access routes through the site, linking up features such as decks or patios, water features, sheds and maintenance areas.
- Pay attention to the neighbourhood and the architecture of the house and consider whether your plans are going to fit in or fight with the existing background.
- When choosing materials, try to define exactly what it is you're after. Is it a hard finish or warm finish that you require in terms of your main surface area? Often we use far too many of the available options in one scheme. There are, of course, exceptions to this rule, but to integrate the garden as a whole, it is easier if your choice of material is kept simple and follows through the entire design.

- Carefully select plant material to take account of your likes and dislikes. Consider, too, factors like children so that you do not introduce any dangerous plants into your scheme – whether they are poisonous or just particularly spiky.
- Make sure that the preferred planting scheme is suitable for your soil and climatic conditions.
- A brand new site can offer a blank canvas. One that is already established, which may have had a few generations of gardens on it, could hold restrictions or be an excellent basis for reinvention. Meditate before removing any existing planting, especially trees that have been established for years. Consider redesigning the garden to use them. Even if they are in an

awkward situation, they could become main players and a new focus in an imaginative design. Are they in any way desirable? Could surgery help? You could take the view that they have more right to be there than your new garden. Sometimes the answer will be obvious from the start. A hideous plant deserves no place and should be whipped out without a moment's bad conscience. You will inevitably want to replace a lot more than you remove.

- Often the designed or planned garden lacks the magic, romance or mystery of one that has just evolved through a process of haphazard planting over a long period or even as a result of semi-neglect. When nature takes its course or where inappropriate planting

occurs, the results can be refreshing, so don't police your garden too strictly – within reason, allow it a little of its own creativity!

- There exist natural laws of proportion, form and their relationships that appear to create balanced compositions that appeal to the human eye. For the garden planner, these are either inherent or can be learned. In technical jargon, they are based on Divine Proportion and the Golden Mean and photographers call it the Principle of Thirds. But the best way to learn about proportion is by careful observation and analysis of a scheme that is pleasing to you or that is well regarded. The secret, however, when using any formula is to disguise it, don't make it obvious. ■

Living

Living

Our relationship with gardens has changed in recent years; whereas once they were for the select few to enjoy, now they are for everybody. This isn't a crime – it's not terrible that gardens aren't all about hard work, cultivation, double digging, manuring, propagation and weeding. Most people's aspiration is for a garden that is a place that they can relax in. Yes, part of that relaxation is nurturing and tending plants, but more and more people are looking towards the end result and how that can be achieved faster and with immense satisfaction. Most of the great garden styles, which we still learn from today, have evolved from the pursuit of pleasure. It seems odd that we now should relegate this to being a by-product of the creation of something beautiful. We shouldn't be ashamed to relax, eat and drink, dance and sing, watch movies and listen to music outside.

Since the 1960s and '70s, the idea of the garden as an outdoor room has gained greater credence. It arrived along with smaller plots – and for the man on the street. Many 'real' gardeners think it's a horrible phrase; how can space that's all to do with cultivation equate with the cosy comfiness of a sitting room, with a television and pictures on the wall? Well, of course it doesn't and it shouldn't mean just that. It means much more, and it's much more important. But a garden needs to have facilities; it needs to have pathways, floors, walls, seating, maybe roofs and possibly entertainment systems. The garden as an outdoor room should be a place that entices people away from their living rooms during the warmer months.

The cry of the traditionalist against the modernist inevitably refers to the latter's use of structure and colour, but even the old-fashioned garden is full of structure – pathways to push wheelbarrows down towards compost heaps, sheds, glasshouses, rockeries, heaven forbid, even patios, and certainly boundaries, walls or fences. The fact that we're used to a traditional form of these structures does not make them any less structural; it is partly because we are used to them that we find them more acceptable than the newer structures of today. If we were to place today's version of the garden shed in a Victorian or Georgian garden, the owners would be outraged with the modernity of the thing. But if something is designed and built well and then planted against – in any style – it surely has a place. Gardens can be a means of fulfilling all sorts of self-expression, not just in planting schemes.

So what do we need outdoors to achieve a certain happiness and ease of use? We need hard surfaces and boundary walls, seats and loungers, football pitches and dog kennels, compost heaps and greenhouses, washing lines and sheds. However, we also want ponds and performing water, buildings as rooms or dens, statuary or ornamental materials, and plants that reflect what we like, not what we're told we should like by the trend masters. We also increasingly want the ability to have sound and vision with television screens or movie projectors, or lighting that's both useful and exciting. We want heat, umbrellas and canopies that protect from the rain or sun – we may even want beds. What we want is a choice of style and of design. We'd love to have the freedom to pick any combination of these desires to create our own space.

We're on the verge of this happening because we realize we're our own bosses and are not guided by purists who tell us what we can and can't do and who has the right to own a garden and to garden in it. Private home ownership, an increase in leisure time and the affluence of society all promote greater democracy in design, and the garden is in the process of being captured as a place to be enjoyed by everyone. For years we've watched the often false and styled lives of others in movies and soap operas, magazines and books and we've come to realize that we can have these things. There's nothing wrong with any form of garden enjoyment; high maintenance, low maintenance, work-based or style-conscious, the garden is there for all who want to seize the opportunity. ■

Jenga

Immerse yourself completely in life outdoors – enjoy the freedom of your garden and of getting wet in it, either deliberately or otherwise.

There is something very primeval about the whole experience of outdoor showering – it brings with it a feeling of being at one with nature, which is, after all, something that many people expect from an outside space. Water is a very important element in every garden – it's essential to all life, be it plant or animal – but it is increasingly being used in garden design in a fun way in addition to its practical usage. When we put an outdoor shower into this garden, it became much more than simply a shower with a practical purpose, we wanted to introduce many other ways of using it too.

The table-top, building game 'Jenga' inspired this garden structure, which in itself made it equally appealing to adults and children alike; for both, it became a climbing frame of mammoth proportions. The fun element of the structure was in the acrylic blocks of primary colour that could be inserted into the walls of the structure to create a bright, stimulating environment for children as well as a vibrant party feel for adults.

The shower room also became a contained, play area for the children. Water is magical for children, as well as having a practical purpose of cooling them down in hot weather and keeping them clean when playing outdoors! Water can, however, be dangerous for children, but by using it in this way, the shower is far safer than a paddling pool since all danger of collected shallow or deep water is removed. The timber decking that was laid as flooring was an ideal choice as it provided a durable, hard-wearing and, most importantly where water is involved, non-slip surface. The shower room was brought right up to date by adding loudspeakers to it. This meant that the children could listen to their own music outside, so it became a really fun place to play in.

But when it came to the adults, the sky was the limit. Whatever the preference for music, be it slow, sensual, hip-grinding blues, or intense and rhythmic dance music, the shower became a playground for the adults too. Obviously the idea of sex in the great outdoors doesn't appeal to everyone, but a simple change of mood music turns the shower room into a place to relax at the weekend or after a hard day at the office. Each of these experiences are all the more heightened by the effect of the water on the herbs planted around the shower area that would release their heady scent as water droplets hit their foliage.

As the room was constructed to be a place to relax in as well as a place for fun, it was important to make it a practical space when a less active pace of life was needed too. In order to accommodate this, we placed wooden sleepers side by side to create raised seating in the middle of the room and also at the side. Instantly the room became a private space to entertain friends – not only during the day, but also in the evening whilst watching the night sky above. For the times when this natural outdoor effect was not wanted, we created a very simple feature for the building – a canvas roof. This roof was offered as an optional addition, and meant that we could introduce another fun aspect to the room or create privacy – with the roof pulled over, the room could become a kid's fort, a private entertaining area or simply a sheltered place in which to enjoy the garden in any weather. ■

Opposite: A self-contained room is constructed from wooden blocks and perspex screens to create a discreet enclosure for an outdooor shower.

Left from top: A massive showerhead creates a sense of jungle romance, while sheets of coloured perspex create privacy during the day and at night turn the enclosed room into a giant, multi-coloured lightbox.

Cylindrical

A party garden doesn't just have to be a night garden, the sense of excitement in the evening can also be gently absorbed into the background during the daytime.

The ultimate extravagance in a garden has to be the creation of a space that is so blatantly for parties – not for kids but for adults.

Of course, adult parties can either begin or end in the evening, so lighting is an important element of creating a party space. As we are increasingly using our gardens in the evenings (especially as this may be the only time we can spend in it during the working week), we are experimenting more with ways to illuminate them and therefore be able to spend the maximum amount of time outdoors. Candles can create a wonderfully relaxing ambience if you want to sit and wind down after a day in the office, or they can provide a gentle flickering glow across a table at dinner. But for this garden, we needed something brighter and more vibrant, something that would get the party going.

We decided to create this atmosphere through the use of copious amounts of neon. Upright, reinforced-steel girder structures were lined with neon, but we also commissioned stand-alone, neon sculptural pieces. With this lighting, any garden can be given the Ibiza-meets-Soho feel, and when these neon lights were used around large, circular decked areas that were laid to imitate dancefloors, this is exactly the feeling that you got. It's perfect – light the barbecue in the evening, invite all your friends around, wait for the sun to go down, turn up the music and, with the flick of a switch, it's party time.

However, as with any form of lighting, do get an expert to install it. If you want lighting, but neon is a little too much for you, there are many other forms of lighting that are now available for your garden, and many you can safely install yourself, such as solar lights. If you do want lighting in your scheme, make sure you incorporate it into your plan in the early stages and remember to lay down any necessary electrical cables before you lay any decking or your patio – you don't want to be digging it all up again later.

Of course, in between the dancing and the partying, a place to sit is pretty important. In this case, we thought that the seating could be used to further enhance the overall look and feel of the garden. We introduced large seating areas with multi-coloured padded cushions that looked surreally like giant chocolate Smarties sunk into the decking. What could make a better chill-out area, after dancing the night away? But for those who wanted to sit and still be part of the party, we devised some swinging chairs at the sides of the deck. These seats perfectly tied in with the nightclub feel, and were hung from the girders of the decking structure, swinging just above the floor, exactly like miniature dancing cages from one of the top Ibiza clubs.

But why not go that one step further? For the ultimate hi-tech party, you could install a screen and projection system, perfect for those psychedelic images shown alongside music at nightclubs. Then, when the partying is over and everyone is lying around chilling on their giant Smarties, you can stick on your favourite old black-and-white movie. ■

Opposite: Strips and squiggles of neon illuminate a series of contained spaces to create a vibrant, party feel.

Below top: Seating need not only be reduced to ground level – explore the potential of hanging hammocks or wooden seats from fixed structures.

Below bottom: Multi-coloured circular cushions are set into the deck to create a seating area with a sense of design and fun.

Curvy

In the lifestyles of both the modern individual or the family, simple, comfortable outdoor spaces play a key part in rest and relaxation.

Seating, even the purists would agree, has to be one of the most important features of a garden. You must be able to go outside and sit down and relax, either for five minutes with a cigarette and a cup of coffee, or after a hard day's toil in the vegetable patch. Your outside space must include places to sit still on your own or in a group. These days the choice of seating is vast; the big retailers have begun to realize that the consumer includes not only those who are prepared to pay for inexpensive plastic furniture, but also those who will invest substantial sums in better designed suites or seats in more durable and sympathetic materials.

When planning and constructing a garden from scratch, you should consider what type of seating you'll want to use in your recreational areas. Sometimes it can be a real pleasure and a bonus to incorporate fixed seats in the overall design, so you're able to build places of relaxation into your hard landscaping framework. Seating can be divided into different categories – fixed seating, which is often built-in; custom-made seating for a special area, or more flexible pieces such as furniture that can be moved around the garden or be taken in and outside at different times of the year.

Another consideration when deciding on seating in the garden is the fact that it can act as a focal point when not in use. The good designer knows that the eye plays funny tricks with the head. If you place a seat in a garden, you're creating an image – and your brain immediately connects that picture with the idea of rest.

This adds to the sense of relaxation in the whole scene and, often, seats and benches are used as devices to indicate peace and tranquillity even if they're seldom, if ever, sat upon.

In this garden, we created a few areas of fixed seating surfaces, some near to the house and others inside the enclosures (see also Enclosures, pp. 158–9). In the enclosed area, a slab of cream-coloured concrete was cantilevered out from a wooden wall. Although the material used was heavy, because the seat was cantilevered – with all the engineering hidden – it gave the impression that it was floating from the wall. The overall effect of this was further enhanced by the soft underplanting directly beneath the seat – not only did we gain the ambience of rest and tranquillity, but the combination of material, form and plants also created a sculptural composition. The softness of the colours of both the wood and the concrete balanced the harder nature of the texture of the seat.

The other seats that we used in this garden were not fixed, but were also made from concrete. This time we used a different type of concrete, which was reinforced but was very slender with flowing lines. Again, the seats looked sculptural, but this time the pieces could be moved around the garden. Despite being made of a hard material, the seats were very comfortable to sit in – they had a relaxing conformation to the back and were low to the ground, which gave a distinct feeling of restfulness. ∎

Opposite: A wooden seat emerges from a wooden wall, appearing to float in a stark but luxurious space.

Above left: Detail is all important; circular spotlights have been integrated into the overall design and work by complementing the structures.

Above right: A slab of white concrete appears to float above a bed of bronze *Heuchera* – magic.

Dotty

Gardens have many jobs to do – so it is important to design a space in which people can use different sections at different times. Good division is the key.

A garden can easily be divided into very clear, separate modules, each of which performs a different function. This can be achieved through shape, structure, content and size. Many of our visits to the garden are fleeting and often functional, and if we have only short pockets of time to use them in our busy lives, we have to work hard to create beautiful gardens that will contain appealing spaces that are easy to use and enjoy.

Dividing the garden into areas of specific use, which might include functional areas just outside the back door, can be a way of planning and utilizing the overall space to its best advantage. Living in the garden may involve dividing a plot into defined sections for assorted functions; it may also mean being able to shut off sections when they're not in use or, indeed, to open up a section at different times during the morning, afternoon or evening for various activities.

In this garden, we had very clear, distinct lines and living areas. Immediately outside the house, we created a deck in a stylized shape. As with most of the features in the garden, it was slightly elevated, and it was fashioned in a combination of wood and stainless steel grid sections. The proximity of the deck to the house allowed the family to easily throw open the back doors at a

moment's notice and wander out to enjoy a cup of tea or a glass of wine within a very defined space without venturing any further into the garden. Although designed and used as a living space, this doesn't mean that the area has to be free of planting; and planting can, in fact, enhance the area. Here, we positioned troughs of iris on the deck which created green architectural interest while also giving a three-dimensional quality to the otherwise flat surface.

The second section of the garden was a softer space that was essentially unconnected to the first, although it could be easily accessed by means of raised wooden ramps. This section was a lawn area and had a different feel and purpose to the decked space. It was an area that could either be just viewed as a carpet or a big block of colour from either end of the garden, to soothe and soften, or as a place to lie down and sunbathe, or even enjoy ball games.

The third section of the garden was more strongly defined than the other two. It was specifically created to be an outdoor room, but one that would serve the dual purpose of also being a light installation. We constructed a square room which was made from metal; its front was painted in vibrant pink with multi-coloured spots that

reflected the colour preferences of the client. Inside the room was an enclosed area, which, during the daytime, could be seen to contain a simple table and chairs as if it were another patio. But when the doors were opened at night, everything changed, and a grid pattern of thirty-six blue lights shone up from the ground to create an amazing show – a specialized light installation.

By adding this touch, the garden could be used in a number of ways for different moods and purposes – we all have different needs and requirements from day to day or even from day to evening, and there is no reason why a garden can't reflect them all. By day or evening the space nearest the house could be a functional living space or a place to relax – an atmosphere enhanced by the rustle of the bamboos planted along the deck – or it could be an extension of the party space below, or the two areas could remain entirely separate, each with a different ambience.

When you start planning a design for your garden, it is important to consider all your different needs – as well as those of others living in the house – and with careful planning you will be surprised at how many of them you can incorporate without having to compromise on style or content. ■

Opposite: A colourful wall creates a dramatic backdrop to a stylish but more sedate garden, but the obvious inclusion of doors lead you to believe there is something beyond – possibly more excitement.

Left: Two modern wicker chairs sit on a slightly elevated patio immediately outside the back door of the house. The strong rectangular lines and the fact that the surface is raised indicate it as a distinct zone.

Stilted

Retreats mean many different things to different people. For some, the images of far off lands could inspire the creation of a place of escape in the garden.

Gardens are, in the main, used as recreational areas and, for many people, recreation really means rest. This idea of rest tends to involve relaxing or reclining, either sitting by a nice warm fire or lying down in a bed – a day bed or a night bed.

European café society has convinced us of the desirability of heat in our outside spaces – an idea that we have embraced very readily with our colder summers. At first, heat was introduced by gas-fired heaters, but, just as the desire for real, log-burning fires in the home has seen a resurgence recently, the real flame of chimineas has become a desirable feature in outdoor spaces. For the same reason, actual fireplaces are also worth considering; in an appropriately sheltered environment, they can be fantastic.

In this garden building, we wanted to include some way of heating the room, but we wanted a more natural look than steel gas heaters, something more in keeping with the wood of the building and the woodland planting beyond. So we incorporated a brick fireplace. It wasn't intended to be the dominant feature, so it was deliberately set at a ninety-degree angle to the house to render it almost invisible from there, but once you were inside the pavilion, it formed the centrepiece. In the evening, a fireplace becomes a natural focus for an individual or for parties of guests to crowd around. Of course, if you like the idea of a fireplace but prefer it to be open-air, you could include a fire pit, which has much the same effect. Sunk down into the ground, it is easy to light and if you build a seating ledge above it, it can be wonderful to sit round on a chilly summer evening.

To echo the flickering flames of the fireplace, we suspended lanterns from the ceiling of the building, which provided gentle, subdued lighting at night and added to the cosy ambience of the room.

Beds (not the horticultural type) can be a fun addition to a garden space and usually need to be enclosed in a covered area – a room, a den or a pavilion. In this garden, the bed was suspended from the ceiling by means of chains. It's a wonderful place to lie in, akin to a hammock, where you can sway and relax and enjoy the view of the garden.

To add a sense of privacy and to shelter the space from the elements, we fitted the longest walls with screens that worked as rolling doors – they could be pushed back or pulled across with ease when needed. The doors functioned separately, so you could close one and not the other depending on the wind direction, or just close one if you wanted to change the view from the building. ■

Opposite: The rectangular room crosses the garden but makes full use of its open sides and the views. The softness of all the reclaimed materials used seems to have a natural home in this environment.

Right: Summer evenings can be made longer by relaxing in front of an open fire.

Far right: Telegraph poles not only keep the building off the ground, but also provide a frame for different views.

High gloss

Ultimate style does not end in a flash restaurant, a smart boutique or in the latest Jaguar – gardens too can be chic, shiny and stylish.

The use of rich, dark-coloured decking, inset with blue-lensed floor lighting, is a great way to give any space a luxurious, vibrant clubby feel – a real sense of *Funk Odyssey* meets *Saturday Night Fever*. This decked area was created with indulgent entertaining very much in mind, and the atmosphere of the space was enhanced by defined areas of sharp-lined furnishings made of wood and steel.

To create a sense of continuity and comfort, we used the same decking that was laid on the ground to clad a very tall, curved, brick retaining wall. Using the same material on the walls and floors provided a smooth flow from ground surfaces to walls and drew the eye upwards to some very high planting above. To break up the wooden walls a little, we inset circular mirrors into them, which allowed the sharp reflections of the seating area to be viewed from many different angles. The mirrors also introduced a different feel to the lighting of the space during the day or evening with natural sunlight or artificial garden lighting, as each would reflect off the mirrors in ever-changing ways. For those evenings when the lighting was not a priority, we also inset a concrete-rendered circle in the wooden wall that could be used as a projection screen.

Planting was an important element of this design as the clients wanted plants to be a strong feature, so that it would be as much a garden as a space for entertaining. In order to achieve this, we built raised beds around the seating area and filled them with plants that either spilled over the edges and softened the texture of the hard landscaping, or rose up at different heights to reflect the levels around the deck.

Mosaic is the perfect material for the garden; it is durable and can be very easy to apply when bought in sheets. From a design point of view, mosaic can be used as an easy means of adding colour, as well as providing an excellent background for the planting scheme. Here, we laid mosaic tiles onto the raised beds, which looked wonderful against the plants – doubly so when it was reflected in the mirrors.

The only other element needed to make this the perfect entertaining area was heat. Rather than introducing a large patio heater that would detract from the rest of the design, we went for a slightly different take and introduced a clean-lined, sleek modern version of the old style braziers, which added the interesting element of real fire to the garden as well as another dimension to the lighting scheme. ∎

Opposite: A luxurious use of colour, texture and furniture all adds up to create this city outdoor dining place.

Below left to right: Deep blue glass lenses are set into a more traditional deck and underlit with fibre optics. For heat, we provided an outdoor fireplace which could be shifted around the garden as the situation required. Glass and tiles, a perfect combination – durable, luxurious and easily maintained.

Case study
Eyes Wide Shut

The garden was a traditional suburban plot, a rectangular space measuring 30 x 9m (100 x 30ft). It had been nicely planted in the past in a traditional manner and had been well maintained in that style. Long, narrow beds ran parallel to the garden fences down both sides, the garden was divided at the centre by a wooden archway and, across and towards the end of the garden, a beech hedge had been fairly recently planted. The only 'features' beyond this hedge were an old shed and a paved area with a compost heap at the very end of the plot. One of the important things to consider when designing or re-designing a garden is what you can retain; clearly, the shed and compost heaps were not top of the list, but there were some existing plants to consider. The main plants that seemed to be of value were an elderly pear tree that arched gracefully above the end of the garden, a magnificent *Pieris*, and a Japanese maple, which had been planted to mark the birth of one of the owners' children.

Case study
Eyes Wide Shut

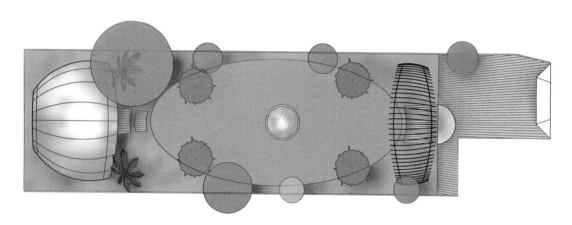

Above left: A very simple plan based on curves creates a gentle overall design which includes a lawn, a central fountain, a steel pergola and a copper room.

Above right: Adding the final touches to the hydraulics opening system for the doorway that is being fixed into place.

Although it was a beautiful garden in a gentle setting, Will and Denise, the owners, didn't feel that it reflected their personalities or their lifestyle. They wanted something more adventurous, something modern, but not overpoweringly so. They liked the idea of symmetry and curved lines, but felt that the current division of the garden did not permit the realization of its full potential. On a practical level, the couple were eager to create a new garden that would serve the needs of a young family, and which would contain interesting planting; but they also wanted an area at the end of the plot that they could entertain in. Soft and contemporary was going to be the on the agenda.

Design and materials

To create a soft feel to the garden, it was important not to echo its rectangular shape by using formal straight lines; instead, the plan centred on using more gentle, oval shapes. Texture would also be important in creating a soft feel, so the main ground-cover area would be laid as a lawn – this was also a good surface and space for the children to play on. Central to the lawn was a concrete bowl that housed a pool of water and a subtle, low-level jet fountain. The use of water is often a tricky element to include in a family garden, as even the smallest amount of water can be dangerous to

unsupervised children. Although small in diameter, the pond was quite deep, so we commissioned a steel grill that could be placed over the top of it to prevent children (or pets) falling in. The grill was removable so that it did not spoil the look of the feature, but could be placed over the water whenever it was needed.

At the far end of the garden, we decided to construct a building in which the couple could entertain; again the structure would be an oval shape to echo the overall design and informal feel of the garden. This structure would be a completely enclosed den which would be glass-fronted, with a central door that would open pneumatically at the flick of a switch. The building was then topped off with a curved, copper roof. I decided on copper, because it is a material that is known for its ever-changing colour: it would start off warm and shiny, but eventually, over time and through exposure to the elements, it would assume the much softer, grey-green tints of verdigris. The building was designed primarily to fit into its landscape and to act as a sleek backdrop to the garden rather than to become a feature that would dominate the space.

We constructed an internal steel skeleton to be used as the frame for the building, but as this would subsequently be clad in wood its beautiful, dramatic structure would be lost. This was

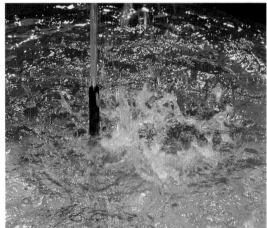

Left: The large opening, the glass, the lines of the steel frame and the sloping decking walkway all invite you in to the garden den.

Above top: Lush planting softened the contemporary design and materials in this garden so that it didn't appear overpoweringly modern.

Above middle: A simple fountain provides an elegant centrepoint to the garden, whether looking from the house or from the pod.

Above bottom: Copper is a wonderful material to use in a garden – it will react with the atmosphere and change its appearance over time.

Case study
Eyes Wide Shut

Above left: Good honest work using familiar tools help to complete the picture.

Above middle and top: *Ilex* 'Golden Gem' and *Acuba japonica* provide some of the main materials at this stage.

Above right: Last-minute sketching clarifies the entrance dimensions and the ramp walkway late in the build.

unfortunate and seemed a shame, and so a second section of the steel skeleton was commissioned which would be used elsewhere in the garden. This second steel frame was then erected as an oval archway at the other end of the lawn, near to the house. This archway would act as an introduction to the garden, serving as a gateway to it, through which one stepped from the traditionally-styled rear of the house into a more modern, sculptural environment. It also acted as a framing device for the view of the lawn, fountain and den beyond while carrying out another function – that of a contemporary trellis.

The steel rungs provided the perfect frame on which to grow climbers, such as the vigorous *Humulus lupulus* 'Aureus', with its vibrant golden foliage, fruiting kiwis (*Actinidia deliciosa* 'Jenny') and an ornamental *Actinidia kolomikta*, with its wonderful green leaves that are tipped with white and pink. The archway looked almost armadillo-like in shape, and the plants were carefully selected so that they would only soften rather than disguise the beauty, drama and modern sculpturalism of the construction.

The architecture and shapes that were incorporated in this garden were inspired by diverse features – from the dashboard of a car to the media pavilion at Lords' cricket ground. Curved shapes can look wonderful and can detract

from the boxey shape of many suburban gardens, but if you are constructing hard landscaping in curved forms, do remember that they can be difficult to achieve in rigid materials. When designing this building, we looked at the construction of traditional European copper domes and translated the techniques used in building them to our copper pavilion, although on a much smaller scale.

We added a hi-tech twist to the building by enabling access to it by means of a central, pneumatically-operated wood and steel door, which swung open magically at the push of a button. Looking out from inside the den, the large single panes of glass on either side of the door gave a feeling of being inside an aquarium and offered a totally different perspective of the garden beyond. At night, the room was illuminated with white lights and blue neon, which, when looking at it from outside, gave it the appearance of hovering slightly above the ground – rather as a space ship might.

Although the two ends of the garden were separated by the lawn, we retained a link and sense of continuity throughout the garden by the pathways at either end of the grass. Both paths were constructed from decking, which was laid out in simple curves – they had a slanted form that invited you to explore further.

Above and above right: An arched framework leads the eye into the garden, echoes the substructure of the pod and acts as a host for climbing plants.

Below and far right: Plants such as Japanese maple, *Dicksonia antarctica* and *Ilex* 'Golden Gem' wait patiently for selection to build up an oasis of foliage.

Right: Nil points to Mr Gavin.

Case study
Eyes Wide Shut

Above and right: Everybody has their job to do as both hard and soft landscaping continue in tandem. While the planting scheme builds up the water dances away merrily and the interior of the pod is fitted out with a soft wooden floor.

Opposite: Looking from the inside out, the completed garden is framed by the eyelashes of our building. Spotlights and neon will play their part in creating an exciting environment at night.

Planting

The design for this garden was intended to be modern, but not overwhelmingly so. In order to ensure the modern materials did not overpower the rest of the garden, we used a subtle, gentle planting scheme to soften the contemporary design of the garden throughout the whole space, not just over the steel archway. Four tall, columnar hornbeams (*Carpinus betulus* 'Fastigiata') were planted symmetrically at the corners of the lawn, which added a degree of formality without being too traditional; they also gave structure and height to the centre of the garden, without seeming to enclose it.

A mixture of shrubby and herbaceous plants enhanced the gentle feel of the garden; evergreens such as *Ilex crenata* and euonymus, and ever-greys, such as santolinas and lavenders, provide winter structure and interest. Spiraeas brought summer colour to the scheme, with masses of white flowers arching gently over the lawn, while clusters of nepetas and geraniums spilled out onto the decking paths.

An exotic touch was added to the garden by planting tree ferns, *Dicksonia antarctica*, of varying heights in front of the copper building; their spectacular leaves mirrored the curves, colours and drama of the building.

Case study
Eyes Wide Shut

Right clockwise from top: *Acer palmatum*, *Lavandula dentata* and *Dicksonia antarctica* used together in this garden create a beautiful combination of texture, foliage and flower.

Selected plant list

Acer palmatum
(Japanese maple) Deciduous shrub/tree. Sun/partial shade, fertile, moist but well-drained soil, shelter from cold winds. H 8m (25ft), S 10m (30ft).

Actinidia deliciosa 'Jenny'
(Chinese gooseberry, Kiwi fruit) Deciduous climber. Self-fertile. Full sun, fertile, well-drained soil. H 10m (30ft).

Actinidia kolomikta
Deciduous climber. Sun, fertile, well-drained soil. H 5m (15ft) or more.

Carpinus betulus 'Fastigiata'
(Hornbeam) Deciduous tree. Sun/semi-shade, well-drained soil, H 15m (50ft) S 12m (40ft).

Dicksonia antarctica
(Tasmanian tree fern) Semi-evergreen fern. Full/partial shade, humus-rich, preferably acid soil. H to 6m (20ft), S 4m (12ft).

Exochorda x macrantha 'The Bride'
(Pearl bush) Deciduous shrub. Full sun/light dapple shade, fertile, moist but well-drained soil. H 2m (6ft), S 1.5m (5ft).

Geranium himalayense 'Gravetye'
(Cranesbill) Herbaceous perennial. Full sun/partial shade, moderately fertile, well-drained soil. H 30cm (12in), S 60cm (24in).

Hemerocallis 'Staghorn Sumach'
Evergreen perennial. Sun, fertile, moist but well-drained soil. H and S 60cm (2ft).

Hosta fortunei var. hyacinthina
Herbaceous perennial. Full/partial shade, fertile, moist but well-drained soil with shelter from cold, drying winds. H 60cm (24in), S 1m (3ft).

Hosta 'So Sweet'
Herbaceous perennial. Full/partial shade, fertile, moist but well-drained soil with shelter from cold, drying winds. H 35cm (14in), S 55cm (22in).

Ilex crenata 'Golden Gem'
(Box-leaved holly) Evergreen shrub. Full sun, moist but well-drained, moderately fertile, humus-rich soil. H 1.1m (3.5ft), S 1.2-1.5m (4–5ft).

Lavandula dentata
Evergreen shrub. Full sun, moderately fertile, well-drained soil. H 1 m (3ft), S 1.5m (5ft).

Ligularia 'The Rocket'
Herbaceous perennial. Full sun with some midday shade, moderately fertile, deep, reliably moist soil. H 1.8m (6ft), S 1m (3ft).

Nepeta 'Six Hills Giant'
(Catmint) Herbaceous perennial. Full sun/partial shade, well-drained soil. H to 90cm (36in), S 60cm (24in).

Paeonia lactiflora 'Sarah Bernhardt'
Herbaceous perennial. Sun/partial shade, deep, fertile, humus-rich, moist but well-drained soil. H and S 90–100cm (36–39in).

Polygonatum humile (syn. P. falcatum)
(Solomon's seal) Herbaceous perennial. Full/partial shade, fertile, humus-rich, moist but well-drained soil. H 20cm (8in), S 50cm (20in) or more.

Rosa rugosa 'Alba'
(White hedgehog rose) Deciduous shrub. Sun, fertile, well-drained soil. H and S 1–2.4m (3–8ft).

Santolina rosmarinifolia
Evergreen shrub. Full sun, poor to moderately fertile, well-drained soil. H 60cm (24in), S 1m (3ft).

Spiraea japonica 'Crispa'
Deciduous shrub. Sun/partial shade, moderately fertile, well-drained soil. H 1.2m (4–5ft), S 1m (3ft).

Spiraea x vanhouttei
Deciduous shrub. Full sun, fertile, moist but well-drained soil. H 2m (6ft), S 1.5m (5ft).

Tiarella cordifolia
(Foam flower). Herbaceous perennial. Deep/partial shade, cool, moist, humus-rich soil. H 10–30cm (4–12in), S to 30cm (12in) or more.

Trollius europaeus
(European globeflower) Herbaceous perennial. Deep, fertile, permanently moisy soil, in sun or partial shade. H 80cm (32in), S 45cm (18in).

Above: Planting and explaining at the same time – the work goes on with or without the cameras.

Right: The completed garden is a soft, contemporary outlook on an outdoor space – eyes wide open.

Dens

Dens

Our primary instinct outdoors is to create shelter for ourselves. The human race didn't land on this planet with houses already built, but as civilization has progressed, we've become very good at creating structures of all scales, from extremely simple shelters to magnificent palaces – wonders of the world, indeed – in which to live, work and play. Having constructed these buildings, however, we still have a desire to inhabit the outdoor spaces beyond them that are undeveloped – having constructed one shelter, we carry on and build more, driven by this primary instinct.

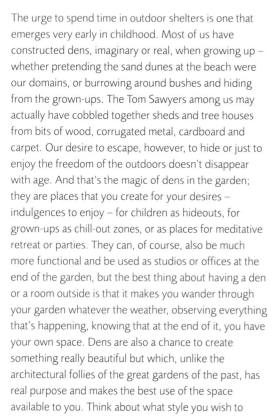

The urge to spend time in outdoor shelters is one that emerges very early in childhood. Most of us have constructed dens, imaginary or real, when growing up – whether pretending the sand dunes at the beach were our domains, or burrowing around bushes and hiding from the grown-ups. The Tom Sawyers among us may actually have cobbled together sheds and tree houses from bits of wood, corrugated metal, cardboard and carpet. Our desire to escape, however, to hide or just to enjoy the freedom of the outdoors doesn't disappear with age. And that's the magic of dens in the garden; they are places that you create for your desires – indulgences to enjoy – for children as hideouts, for grown-ups as chill-out zones, or as places for meditative retreat or parties. They can, of course, also be much more functional and be used as studios or offices at the end of the garden, but the best thing about having a den or a room outside is that it makes you wander through your garden whatever the weather, observing everything that's happening, knowing that at the end of it, you have your own space. Dens are also a chance to create something really beautiful but which, unlike the architectural follies of the great gardens of the past, has real purpose and makes the best use of the space available to you. Think about what style you wish to

achieve, whether it be formal, traditional, contemporary, wacky, or country-cottage cosy.

Materials

Durability of any outside structures is very important and will influence the materials you choose for your construction. The main enemy of different substances when used outside is water, which tends to destroy many materials unless they are properly treated. Obviously in a garden, water is also our biggest friend, so to build and create you have to be aware of the destructive power of the environment. Along with water, sunlight, variations in temperature and wind turbulence can all wreak havoc.

If you want to transcend an assumed quality of form, if you are looking to create an effect that enjoys strength but also has a lightness of touch, keep your eyes open and look for new interpretations of conventional building materials. Even common materials seen in a different light can provide good and honest architectural interest. Corrugated steel and aluminium are interesting examples; we are used to seeing them on a run-down shed or on the roof of outbuildings, but used alone, they have an integrity that allows their inherent strengths to shine. In the past, I've used corrugated metal to clad a very modern art studio that appeared to float over a

large, still pond. In this situation, it was transformed into a glowing box by using a rubberized yellow paint, but even if left raw and shiny or simply sealed, corrugated metal can provide a dramatic statement.

Recently, I have been favouring wood more and more. Many timbers are durable in their natural form; western red cedar, for example, has its own natural oil preservatives and most timbers can easily be treated to make them last. Salvaged woods, such or railway sleepers and telegraph poles, have real character and history and make great building blocks for the construction of elegant garden buildings of real substance. Wooden buildings also have the advantage of being classified as temporary structures under planning law – if they are below a certain size – and are therefore exempt from planning permission. But best of all, wooden structures seem to merge seamlessly into a garden setting – organic in origin, they just belong outside.

So let's open our eyes to the possibilities – dens are simply places in a garden setting that have a range of uses and can be built from myriad materials and inspired by a variety of ideas. From copper to flint stone, from slate to stainless steel, from glass to brick, dens are built for many purposes – retreats, offices, spiritual places, family rooms and children's playhouses – and they can find a place in any garden. ■

Miami

Modern, clean-lined, sleek and white – an open contemporary garden structure that looks forward as well as looking back.

Modern and simple with clean, straight lines in white concrete and glass. These were the rules for the overall design of the garden, but one of the primary requirements was to create some shelter – a space outdoors for relaxing. The only thing that worried me was the potential for the garden as a vista, as there was a lovely view from the house as the garden level rose gently towards the back. I didn't want to lessen the impact of the length of the plot, or detract from the feeling of space by enclosing any part of it. So, the design that evolved was for a garden room fairly near the house that would remain open so that it would frame the views of what was beyond. To achieve this, the building itself wasn't enclosed – although curtains could be dropped from integrated boxes at the front and back of the structure to give a sense of privacy, if needed. The idea of openness and framing continued throughout the design, and rather than creating two solid sides to the building, glass brick walls were built in a frame of white concrete pillars so that light could invade from all sides, while the poured concrete roof provided shelter from the sun and rain.

The overall feeling of the building was 1930s Miami Beach architecture, but it was also slightly reminiscent of London Underground architecture in its use of modernist materials, often painted white with inset lines of blue glass hiding neon lights. White stone was used for the patio steps and the room flooring, but the hard surface was softened by cushions set around low seating areas and a simple coffee table.

The overall idea behind the design was to create a space that would celebrate light and allow views of the simple architecture. One could imagine large groups of people sitting on the different levels of the steps enjoying barbecues, and children playing in the grassed area beyond the pavilion. All the planting around the structure was contained in low, trough-like beds of rendered block, which were also painted white. The structure was set as an island in a lawn – the green turf contrasting starkly with the brilliant white of the hard landscaping. Televisions or music systems could be plugged in for outdoor entertainment, but this building would never look cluttered. Even in mid-winter, when it wasn't being used, the pavilion would frame the view beyond it and make a welcome addition to an open landscape. ■

Opposite: Level changes play an important part in creating gentle excitement. The room is stepped with the centrepiece being a simple, elegant table. The openings at the front and back of the building lead to even more steps which can be used as tiered seating or as access to the garden beyond.

Above: Despite the use of glass brick and lots of concrete, the overall impression is of softness and light.

Left: The structure is an open one and, although quite near the house, allows a framed vision of the planting beyond.

Stilted

Sometimes gardens are too beautiful to touch. The secret can be stepping over what already exists and building above it; without damaging a blade of grass or the sense of nature.

The primary function of this structure was to provide a space that would promote relaxation and an appreciation of the surroundings. It was designed as a platform, albeit an enclosed platform or, rather, a platform that housed an enclosure. The idea was to create a space within an already beautiful garden setting that just enhanced the enjoyment of the surroundings. The garden itself was very simple but beautiful and contained mature specimen trees, including cedar and willow, at the back of the plot, which lent a woodland feel.

The garden pavilion was designed so as not to detract from the existing spirit of the location. It would be a screened building that would travel across the rectangular shape and be held above the ground on stilts. The position of the retreat was determined by the cedar tree and the structure was devised in rectangular form, with a series of eight telegraph poles sunk into the ground around which the framework for the building was built.

The client wanted the building to have the feel and style of a Moroccan hideaway. Transferring this to English suburbia is not without difficulties, so the essence of the style was achieved mainly in the way the room was furnished. But a number of other influences can be readily seen with a pavilion of this sort – the most obvious is that of a Japanese tea house, in that moveable screens at the front and back of the building framed views and created privacy and intimacy when needed. The principles of Indonesian architecture were clear in the elevation of the structure, but it could also be said

that the flat nature of the building – a simple rectangular box – owed something to domestic American architecture of the 1950s.

The materials used for construction were chosen on the basis that they would be in keeping with the overall sylvan nature of the site. The relationship that people have with various materials is very different. For a spiritual person, the use of reclaimed wood in this situation could be significant – most of the elements of this structure had a former life: the telegraph poles had previously supported communication wires, the floor and ceiling wood were all reclaimed, and even the bricks for the fireplace had had a former existence in an old house. By their very origin and nature, all these materials had character. Another important factor for the whole ambience of the room was that the wood flooring was warm to the touch and the materials could be enjoyed barefoot. A large pane of glass was set into the roof which allowed natural light to stream in, whilst also allowing the user of the room to look up and appreciate the arching branches of the grey cedar above.

When all the wood and mesh panels were pushed back, the room became nothing more than a raised, covered platform that acted as an introduction to the rest of the garden beyond. In order to reflect the informal and natural feel of the already stunning garden, the planting scheme here was extremely simple – just a few ferns set in at angles at the base of mature trees. Sometimes, simplicity is key. ∎

Opposite: Existing trees in the garden determined where our building would go. An outdoor haven was created as a place to relax in, but also a place to be near what was already there. A bed hanging from chains within the house enhances the sense of relaxation.

Above left: Wood and metal screens slide along rails to open and close off views or to create a sense of privacy.

Above centre: Everything is suspended off the wooden poles which are set into the ground at the end of the garden.

Above right: A fireplace adds to the feeling of the den as a comfortable retreat.

Rapunzel

An outdoor building need not only provide a practical space, but it can also be the major focal point, the item that gives you an immediate sense of what your garden is all about.

I have a liking for contemporary materials and for exploring the use of materials and structures that are not normally seen in gardens, often drawing on outside influences for their design. This situation, however, demanded a backward glance – a look at the past history and architecture of a small garden. This site was very old and had once contained a building that had been used commercially for a range of skills over the years. The workshop that existed was not a listed building, had no inherent architectural beauty and was dominating a small site, but although we needed to redress the balance of the garden and give more room over to outdoor living and plants, it seemed a shame to have to remove it completely. So instead, rather than just destroy it, I decided to create something new out of something old and to rebuild the structure in the garden in a slightly different way, but by using the salvaged material from the building.

Traditionally, all manner of buildings were constructed from local materials, thus giving them the effect of emerging from, rather than being imposed on, the surrounding landscape. In this instance, we used old flint and brick; they are materials that have soul and history and which also naturally blend in with the garden setting while providing a fantastic backdrop for plants. The gently pitched roof was traditionally tiled and topped with a lead hat.

There were some practical considerations when reconstructing this building, we needed to replace the storage space that we had removed with the old structure, so a new building of a more pleasing and integrated shape was needed. As this structure would also act as a final focal point in the enlarged area, I designed a simple tower that would be settled into a corner. Its romantic quality would be reflected in the proposed new planting scheme, including climbing roses that would clamber from the base of the building (see Planting, pp.104–5). I wanted to create the overall impression that the tower had been there for generations so that it would really blend into the garden, and so the romantic element was not just confined to the planting, but was also inherent in the small windows that evoked castles and turrets of times long past. The finished tower echoed the strong circular theme in the garden and was in proportion to the rear garden of a small, Victorian, end-of-terrace house.

The tower, which looked like it was drawn from the illustrated pages of *Grimm's Fairy Tales*, was a magic place for children to play in and exercise their imagination. It evoked *Dungeons and Dragons*, Rapunzel, Sleeping Beauty and even Harry Potter. Providing a den for the children is about keeping all members of the family happy – and what better way to encourage them into the garden than by providing their own hideaway from the grown-ups? And, of course, adults are happy to see children playing instead of glued to the TV or computer games. But just because it's for the children doesn't mean it can't also be beautiful in its own right and work as an aesthetic focal point for the garden. ◼

Opposite: A circular tower with a tiled roof, constructed from local materials, creates a sense of romance and fairytales.

Above left to right: Lavender, roses and hibiscus will all justify a little bit of tender care with months of profuse flowering.

Torpedo

A building can be designed to fit in subtly with its surroundings or to stand out in a bold and beautiful way. Simple lines often create the best design.

A garden room can be multi-functional, but given the fast pace of modern living, relaxation seems to be a high priority for many people. But, inevitably, this doesn't always suit everyone and some outdoor rooms need to reflect the individual tastes and needs of more than one person. This garden room had to do just that and be a place for all the family – somewhere for entertainment and stimulation, as well as a place to chill out and relax. But this den also had to be a place that was slap bang in the middle of the garden, from where you could enjoy the beauty of the new planting that was unfolding all around.

As the overall plan for the garden was to be inspired by simple modernity, I wanted to reflect this in the structure of the building, creating strong lines and curves that mirrored those of the rest of the garden and the architectural, easy and interesting planting. Inspiration came from Danish designer Arne Jacobson's furniture – especially his chairs with their beautiful shapes, elegant form, functional comfort and innovative construction. The building was constructed so that it would appear to be floating above the garden – overhanging the raised beds around it and supported by a single, almost invisible pole. The overall shape of the building was formed by straight lines with c-shaped curves at either end, rather like the caterpillar tracks of a JCB; it was constructed in steel and wood with large expanses of glass forming the walls on each side.

The space was large enough to satisfy everyone's needs. At one end of the room, a hot tub was installed, which was only revealed as and when it was needed by lifting part of the floor. The furniture was carefully chosen to reflect the style of the building, there wasn't much of it – simplicity was key. The egg chair in a glass frame was almost an installation when viewed from outside. This room was a place to relax, to ponder, to play chess and a place from which to admire the garden. You could enjoy the hot tub or watch TV, move a table in and have dinner with your friends, or even just simply enjoy its form from the outside. ■

Opposite: Our transparent room is raised on a single, steel beam and frames an elegant piece of furniture, but it also appears to gather up the majestic trunks of the trees beyond. It is a large building but, because of the broad use of glass, it is see-through and appears to blend into the landscape.

Below left to right: The building, although limited in space, is truly multi-functional – even a hot tub is revealed below the floorboards.

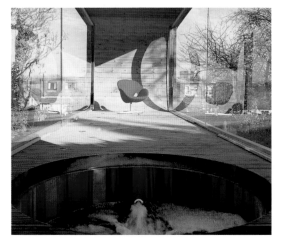

Poles apart

Dens needn't be fully enclosed structures – it is also possible to create intimate spaces simply by defining boundaries and roofing over them.

When is a garden building not a building? A den doesn't need to be an enclosed structure. It could be just a platform – a raised platform with or without a roof – that gives a feeling of enclosure, elevation or even a feeling of a lookout post.

In creating a meditative retreat, as here, you might want to consider whether or not you need walls, or even a roof. By constructing a building with open sides, you can allow the views from beyond to become a feature of the space and gain atmospheric effects within the space from the mood of the planting that surrounds it. An open-sided structure like this is also much easier to integrate into the overall landscape. Similarly, sitting in a structure that is open to the power of the elements, or even one that is enclosed but with glass walls or roof, can create an appropriate space for cosmic contemplation. Stainless steel, fibreglass and coloured concrete are not particularly spiritual materials, unlike wood, which, for some of us, appears to have a soul of its own. We created this building from wood, with nine telegraph poles for uprights, so that the open-sided pavilion had the feel of a temple – quiet, calm and reflective – with floors decked in smooth wood that invited you to walk barefoot upon it.

The pavilion was in a prominent position at the end of the garden and so the roof was also clad to make it more appealing to the overlooking neighbours. The telegraph pole uprights created cohesion, within and without the garden, as they echoed the upright trunks of the newly planted and existing trees. Sitting inside the pavilion, or indeed lying in the suspended hammock, you could appreciate the fusion of planting in an East-meets-West style – the juxtaposition of the Japanese maples and azaleas beside the native birches. A low-slung box, reminiscent of ceremonial Japanese tea tables, and a simple construction of two raised sleepers doubled as seating or tables.

In this garden, Zen-like minimalism, clean lines and purity created a place that was still and contemplative and at one with nature. ▪

Opposite: An open pavilion with simple furniture is the focal point. Sitting in here you can look back towards the house at a succession of simple, cubed rooms which step up the slope.

Below: A hammock is the perfect accessory in a peaceful garden – you can sway gently from a covered position and read your book, or just enjoy your paradise.

Case study
Egghead

Very often, people buy their houses because they love the garden, and so get very frustrated when they don't know what to do with it to fulfil its potential. This garden was to be built for a young couple who lived in a suburban estate outside London. They had bought their home because of the garden and because they wanted space for their two children. They were very definite about their ideas and their likes and dislikes for the outside space and they knew that they wanted something modern but not scary, something exciting and colourful and something that would be made from quality materials. But above all, they wanted a space that could be enjoyed by all the members of the family – a safe place for excitement and entertainment, a truly modern garden.

Case study
Egghead

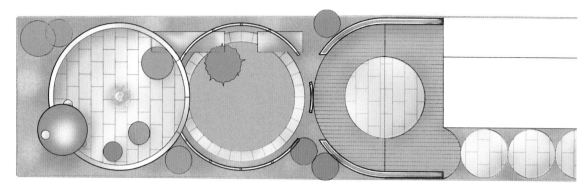

Right: Circles are used as a device to break up the space and create enclosures that can be used by different people at different times of the day for different activities.

Opposite: The cylindrical wooden tunnels provide a safe, fun route through the garden for the children.

This site was already appealing to a gardener; it was an average-sized garden with relaxed borders running down the left- and right-hand sides that were crammed with old-fashioned shrubs such as viburnums, buddlejas, hydrangeas and old roses; and there was an old, established apple tree in the lawn. Beyond the garden was a young willow tree, and after that, a cricket pitch. But what really defined the site were the massive open skies – really clear and beautiful. It was not a level garden – there was a fall of about a metre (3ft) from top to bottom, and this was a factor that would come into play in the design.

The design

The concept for this garden evolved from the idea of creating rooms from interlocking circles. At the far end of the garden, a completely circular room with opening doors was designed as a space that could be closed off from the outside world. This room was constructed on a metal frame, with a double wooden cladding of western red cedar that enclosed a relatively spacious void. This allowed for all manner of technology and fittings to be incorporated internally, adding to the sleek-finished feel of the overall project. The centrepiece of this room, built into the walls, was a giant egg made of rendered brick. This egg was painted purple and was finished off with Perspex dome windows and an oval, steel, mirror-effect door. The egg was intended to act as a shed, projection room and housing for a stereo unit that would power an integrated speaker system. Surround-sound was built into the curved frame of the walls. An audio-visual surveillance system was also installed so that two cameras could observe all that was happening and transmit pictures of the children at play to a camera on top of the refrigerator in the client's kitchen.

The floor of the room at the end of the garden was laid with grey Indian sandstone and the circular lawn that housed the old apple tree became the other main ground cover. The sandstone continued throughout the garden

Case study
Egghead

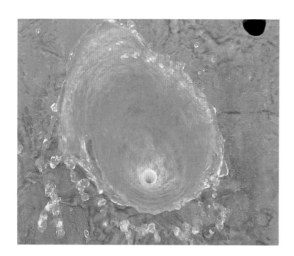

Opposite: An egg made from brick, which was rendered and painted lavender, works as a multi-functional space set within circular walls of an enclosed courtyard. It acts a projection room, light source and a garden shed.

Left top to bottom: Water contained in an underground reservoir spurts up at the touch of a button. Brightly coloured children's toys find the perfect home in this setting while built-in lighting appears to be strips of vibrant colour during the daytime.

Bottom: The brilliant team of builders and carpenters that make these gardens happen.

as a circular pathway and these circular details were repeated in the wooden decking near the house and in the rings of Perspex lights that were held in place with bands of mirror-finished stainless steel. This light added a magical effect in the evening and the stripes of blue, orange and red created a warm, surrounding glow. The egg contained its own magic, with lengths of fibre-optics creating a continuous glowing and flowing of many different colours that could be seen through the Perspex openings.

The entrance from this room into a second circular room was through a set of double doors; the outline of the room was formed by a skeleton

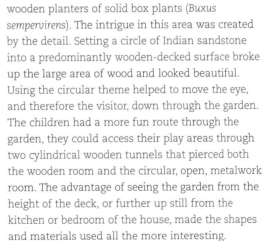

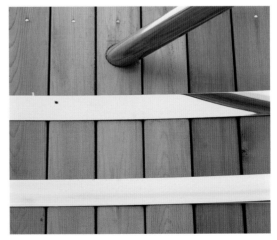

of stainless steel reinforcement bars, welded together in a mish-mash pattern. The idea here was to create the sense of the wall as a sculpture, while, at the same time, re-working the idea of creating trelliswork out of modern, unusual materials. The reinforcing bars created a framework, 200mm (8in) thick, that supported newly planted climbing plants and also let existing plants peep through. Ten blue lights were situated at the base of the framework, which created blue-tinged reflections from the metalwork at night, in effect creating a giant circular lantern.

Semi-circular decks led on two levels from the back of the house, which incorporated raised wooden planters of solid box plants (*Buxus sempervirens*). The intrigue in this area was created by the detail. Setting a circle of Indian sandstone into a predominantly wooden-decked surface broke up the large area of wood and looked beautiful. Using the circular theme helped to move the eye, and therefore the visitor, down through the garden. The children had a more fun route through the garden, they could access their play areas through two cylindrical wooden tunnels that pierced both the wooden room and the circular, open, metalwork room. The advantage of seeing the garden from the height of the deck, or further up still from the kitchen or bedroom of the house, made the shapes and materials used all the more interesting.

Despite the modern materials used in the hard landscaping and structures, the planting style was not to be modern; instead, it would incorporate many of the existing plants. But the new plants that we would add to the garden were to be soft, avoiding structured, architectural planting. In the furthest space – the wooden room – the paving slabs were lifted to create islands of growth amongst them: a beautiful Japanese maple (*Acer palmatum*) arched over the entrance tunnel, while a copper beech (*Fagus sylvatica* Atropurpurea Group) framed a view of the egg. Squares of iris, thyme, grasses, skimmia and herbaceous perennials created a light checkerboard effect and softened the

Left: Reinforced stainless steel bars create a sculptural wall and a climbing frame for a host of plants.

Below: Constructing the crawl-through space.

Opposite page from left: The purple flower of this *Iris sibirica* 'Silver Edge' looks stunning against the lavender wall of the egg. Planting such as these grasses and hydrangeas softens the hard edges of the wooden tunnel and creates a jungle effect for the children as they climb through it.

stone and wood surroundings. By creating individual planting holes for these plants, we could successfully incorporate soil types and conditions suitable for the individual nurture of the particular plants, which in turn allowed us to select from a wider variety.

In the second section of the garden, we planted climbers, such as actinidia, golden hop (*Humulus lupulus* 'Aureus'), clematis and roses, and underplanted them with hydrangeas, ferns, grasses, hostas, ligularias, euonymus, achilleas and anemones to give bursts of colour and form all year round. ∎

Selected plant list

Achillea 'Moonshine'
(Yarrow) Herbaceous perennial.
Full sun, moist but well-drained
soil. H and S 60cm (24in).

**Aralia elata
'Aureovariegata'**
(Japanese angelica tree)
Deciduous tree. Fertile, humus-
rich, moist soil in an open or
partially shaded site, sheltered
from strong winds.
H and S 15m (15ft).

**Berberis thunbergii f.
atropurpurea**
(Barberry) Deciduous shrub.
Full sun/partial shade, almost
any well-drained soil.
H 1m (3ft), S 2.5m (8ft).

Buxus sempervirens
(Common box) Evergreen
shrub. Partial shade, fertile,
well-drained soil. H 5m (15ft),
S 5m (15ft) or more.

**Campanula lactiflora
'Loddon Anna'**
Herbaceous perennial. Sun or
light shade, fertile, moist but
well-drained, neutral to alkaline
soil. H 1.2–1.5m (4–5ft),
S 60cm (24in).

Clematis 'Alice Fisk'
Deciduous climber. Full sun,
with roots in shade in fertile,
humus-rich, well-drained soil.
H 2–2.4m (6–8ft), S 1m (3ft).

Clematis 'Rouge Cardinal'
Deciduous climber. Full sun,
with roots in shade in fertile,
humus-rich, well-drained soil.
H 2–3m (6–10ft), S 1m (3ft).

Digitalis ferruginea
(Rusty foxglove)
Biennial/perennial. Partial
shade, humus-rich soil, but will
tolerate most soils and
situations except very wet and
very dry. H to 1.2m (4ft),
S 45cm (18in).

**Dryopteris filix-mas
'Linearis Polydactyla'**
Deciduous fern. Partial shade,
sheltered site, moist humus-rich
soil. H 60cm (24in).
S 38cm (15in).

**Euonymus fortunei
'Emerald 'n' Gold'**
Evergreen shrub. Full sun,
any soil, including poor ones.
H 60cm (24in), S 90cm (36in).

**Fagus sylvatica
Atropurpurea Group**
(Copper beech) Deciduous
tree. Full sun, tolerant of a wide
range of well-drained soils,
including chalk. H 25m (80ft),
S 15m (50ft).

**Geranium sanguineum
'Max Frei'**
Herbaceous perennial. Sun or
partial shade, in any moderately
fertile, well-drained soil.
H 20cm (8in), S 30cm (12in).

**Hemerocallis
'Stella de Oro'**
(Daylily) Evergreen perennial.
Sun, fertile, moist but well-
drained soil. H 30cm (12in),
S 45cm (18in).

**Hydrangea macrophylla
'Soeur Therese'**
Deciduous shrub. Sun/partial
shade with shelter from cold,
drying winds, moist but well-
drained, moderately fertile,
humus-rich soil.
H and S 1.5m (5ft).

Iris sibirica 'Silver Edge'
Herbaceous perennial. Sun or
light shade, fertile, moist but
well-drained soil. H and S
50–120cm (20–48in).

Ligularia przewalskii
Perennial. Full sun with some
midday shade, moderately
fertile, deep, reliably moist soil.
H to 2m (6ft), S 1m (3ft).

Lonicera henryi
(Honeysuckle) Evergreen
climber. Full sun/partial shade,
fertile, humus-rich, moist but
well-drained soil.
H and S 10m (30ft).

Luzula nivea
(Snowy woodrush) Evergreen
perennial rush. Full sun, poor to
moderately fertile, humus-rich,
reliably moist but well-drained
soil. H to 60cm (24in),
S 45cm (18in).

**Luzula sylvatica
'Marginata'**
(Greater woodrush) Evergreen
perennial rush. Deep/partial
shade, poor to moderately
fertile, humus-rich, moist but
well-drained soil. H to 70–80cm
(28–32 in), S 45cm (18in).

**Miscanthus sinensis
'Rotsilber'**
Perennial grass. Full sun,
moderately fertile, moist but
well-drained soil. H 2m (4ft).

**Paeonia lactiflora
'Karl Rosenfield'**
(Peony) Herbaceous perennial.
Full sun/partial shade, deep
fertile, humus-rich, moist but
well-drained soil. H and S
70–80cm (28–32in).

Parthenocissus henryana
(Virginia creeper) Deciduous
climber. Shade or sun, but best
in partial shade in fertile,
well-drained soil.
H and S 10m (30ft).

**Persicaria bistorta
'Superba'**
(Bistort) Semi-evergreen
perennial. Full sun/partial
shade, prefers moist soil but will
tolerate dry soil. H and
S 90cm (36in) or more.

Rosmarinus officinalis
(Rosemary) Evergreen shrub.
Full sun, well-drained, poor to
moderately fertile soil. H and S
1.5m (5ft).

**Sedum 'Herbstefreude'
(syn. S. Autumn Joy)**
Herbaceous perennial. Full sun,
moderately fertile, well-drained,
neutral to slightly alkaline.
H and S to 60cm (24in).

Uncinia rubra
(Hook sedge) Evergreen
perennial sedge. Full sun/light
dappled shade, moderately
fertile, humus-rich, moist but
well-drained soil. H 30cm
(12in), S 35cm (14in).

**Viburnum opulus
'Roseum'**
(Snowball tree)
Deciduous shrub. Full
sun/partial shade, any
moderately fertile, moist
but well-drained soil.
H and S 4m (12ft).

Planting

Planting

Getting my hands in the soil and planting is always my favourite part of the work I do on *Home Front in the Garden.* Although it is usually the last job I do on a build – once all the big constructions are in place and the site is clear – it's the one that I find the most exhilarating and enjoyable. In some gardens the planting scheme can be deliberately architectural or intended to be the main focus, but in others it is the hard landscaping which provides structure and a skeleton for the design. In both situations, though, this is the time that the plants work their magic, for it is plants that really bring a design alive and make a space a garden.

Plants with purpose

Plants are used in the garden for many different purposes. When laid out in swathes or blocks, plants can be arranged to draw your eye in a particular direction through the garden so that your attention is drawn to different areas of the garden, or directly to a focal point. Plants may, of course, be the focal points themselves, as in mature specimen trees and shrubs, or when grown in large pots. Similarly, plants can enhance the structure of a design by adding height or an architectural element to the garden with their bold forms. They also serve the important purpose of softening hard landscaping and structures, or of adding bright, dramatic splashes of colour. Taller plants such as trees and bamboos can make indispensable screens and boundaries around the edge of the garden to provide some privacy, or they can integrate the garden with areas outside its boundaries, for example, by framing views of landscapes beyond. Your choice of plants can also determine or help create the style of the garden, be it contemporary, cottage, formal, Mediterranean, Japanese, Italian, prairie style or jungle, or can define the mood – calming and cooling, or hot and tropical.

Carefully planning and deciding on your planting scheme can dictate whether your garden will be high or low maintenance. The maintenance level you require will depend on your interest and the amount of time available to you to spend in the garden (see p.21). Many herbaceous plants do need staking, dividing or pruning and they can be high maintenance. And while subtropical exotics may seem easy – with no pruning needed – they do need the special care of wrapping with fleece or moving to warm spots in the winter to ensure they survive the frosts. Trees and shrubs tend to be the lower maintenance members of the garden, although they still require a certain amount of attention, particularly in the early years. To my mind, low maintenance is often soulless and boring – good things require care and the effort you put in will be rewarded. Plus, gardening is a fun and relaxing activity and can be very therapeutic after a long day at work!

The right site

Of course, in some respects, it doesn't matter how you express your taste in plants in the garden – if you haven't got suitable soil for the particular plant, it just is not going to do well. Choose the plants carefully to suit your site. For example, in wet, boggy areas, use moisture-loving birch or alder, and for shady areas, use ferns instead of trying to force sun-lovers to perform. Not all plants will grow all over the UK, but don't let this dishearten you – each area has its own star plants: for instance, the Himalayan blue poppies (*Meconopsis*) do particularly well in Scotland, while palms and more succulent plants are more suitable for warmer, more southerly gardens.

So you need to know your soil type, and you can find out if it's clay, sandy or loam by feel. Clay will stay firm in your hand when compressed and take a polished finish if you rub it, sandy soils feel gritty and will not hold together when squeezed, while loam is the perfect mix of the two. Once you've established the structure, then assess its pH level. If you don't know whether your soil is acidic or alkaline, take a peek at what's growing in your neighbour's garden – if there are lots of flourishing rhododendrons that will be a good indicator that it is an acid soil. If that doesn't give you the answer you need, go to your local garden centre and buy a soil pH tester – they are very easy to use and will give you an accurate idea of what you have to work with. And remember, however nutritionally poor your soil is, it can always be improved by a good wheelbarrow-load of horse manure or garden compost.

Placing and finding plants

Once you've decided on the theme and style of your planting scheme, draw up a careful planting plan with all your preferred plants where they would be happiest. Once you've established what and how many of each you want, it's time to go shopping. Local garden centres and nurseries should be your first port of call – not just for convenience, but also because the chances are they will be selling plants that are proven to survive and thrive in your local situation and climate. If you've really got your heart set on that one particular plant and you can't find it, don't despair – for more unusual purchases you may have to check out mail order catalogues or the internet, or get a copy of the Royal Horticultural Society's annual publication, *Plant Finder*, which will tell you your nearest supplier of a particular plant. ∎

Hovercraft

When the overall theme of the garden is fairly exotic, with influences being taken from all sorts of obscure areas, the planting can easily follow suit.

When you have very strong dominant horizontal lines, such as the terraced decking in this garden, you often need to add some vertical interest and lead the eye skywards. Italian terraced gardens are frequently dotted with the Italian cypress, *Cupressus sempervirens*. These beautiful evergreen trees are great architectural plants; their form makes an excellent punctuation mark in any garden and they stay pencil thin – so you get good height that doesn't take up much ground space in the garden. For a deciduous option, try out *Carpinus betulus* 'Fastigiata'. Other slim-line conifers include the Irish yew, *Taxus baccata* 'Fastigiata' and, for small gardens, the dwarf *Thuja occidentalis* 'Smaragd'. The butter-yellow stems of the coppiced *Salix alba* subsp. *vitellina* provide winter colour.

It's not just trees that can provide great vertical drama – the biennial *Echium pininana* will reach for the sky with amazing blue spires of flowers. Bamboos, such as the phyllostachys used here, will also counterbalance the strong horizontal lines with their tall stems and airy, light-textured foliage. Depending on your preference, you can have the exotic colours of the black-stemmed *Phyllostachys nigra*, or the yellow-stemmed *P. aurea*. The lower-growing, mound-forming bamboos, such as *Sasa*

veitchii, are also good choices, but watch out, as, like many bamboos, sasa can be invasive if not kept in check.

Fan-shaped and sword-like leaves will also break up flat lines. On the top deck, we used Chusan palm, *Trachycarpus fortunei* – the fan-shaped, evergreen leaves provide a bold outline and touch of the tropics. The dwarf fan palm, *Chamerops humilis*, which also comes in a silver form (*C. humilis* var. *argentea*), would also be a gorgeous tropical choice. Bunches of sword-shaped leaves, such as those of *Cordyline australis* and phormiums, will add energy to a scheme, or for something a little different, try a silver-leaved *Astelia chathamica*. Hurtling through the foliage were tall red-hot pokers; *Kniphofia caulescens* has thick, fleshy, succulent leaves that are stouter and more upright than other kniphofias, which tend to flop around. In a similar vein, use *Crocosmia* 'Lucifer', the lower-growing montbretia, *Crocosmia* x *crocosmiiflora*, *Iris pallida* 'Variegata' or *Sisyrinchium striatum*, which is a semi-evergreen perennial producing slender spikes of creamy-yellow flowers in summer.

Agave americana 'Variegata' was dotted around in pots on the decks and formed a unifying link between the different levels. Its weird spiky form is like a sculpture carved from green- and cream-striped rock and is

extremely eye-catching. It acts as a magnificent focal point. If you don't like variegated plants, try the plain green *Agave americana*. Other weird and wonderful plants of a similar outline include yuccas, aloe, and *Beschorneria yuccoides*, all of which will grow in the south of England in a sheltered position. *Pseudopanax ferox*, which has a slightly alien and menacing aura, would also be a great talking point and object of curiosity.

Grasses added texture, height and mass to this scheme. The *Cupressus sempervirens* was underplanted with curls of the bronze form of *Carex comans*, while fountains of *Cortaderia selloana* and *Stipa gigantea* emerged from various positions around the decks.

The harsh horizontal and vertical lines are softened by low-growing mounds and soft hummocky shapes. Here I used the evergreen *Pittosporum tobira* 'Nanum', which has glossy, dark green foliage and forms a compact, rounded mound, with the added bonus of intensely scented white flowers. Other possibilities are *Viburnum davidii* which also has glossy, evergreen foliage and a compact habit, but larger, more striking leaves. The rounded perennial, *Euphorbia polychroma* adds vibrant acid-green bracts. If something larger is required, try the wonderful *Euphorbia characias* subsp. *wulfenii*. ∎

Left to right: Colour and form can be achieved from foliage as well as flowers. The delicate sprays of the *Cortaderia selloana*, the striped leaves of the *Agave americana* 'Variegata' and the golden colour of the *Salix alba* subsp. *vitellina*.

Opposite: *Agave americana* 'Variegata', *Cordateria* and *Stipa* combine to work against the new structures, vying with them to be noticed first. Much of the planting in this garden took place either on the steep slope or in containers positioned on the platforms.

Curvy

The initial request from the client for this garden was for luxury in both materials and in planting. Dark foliage plants reflected the sensual mood of the space.

Sensual, sexy and luxurious are the keynotes for this planting scheme with moody and lush undertones. The plants look beautiful against the warm cedar walls that create the two separate courtyards, unified by a large cherry tree in the centre. The planting was also very specific in terms of colour tones, as the client had requested black plants. However, genuinely black plants are quite rare and plants that are described as black are often, on closer inspection, very dark red or purple. But a visit to the amazing gardens of dark plants specialist, Derry Watkins, in Wiltshire, turned out to be a treasure trove of dusky delights. Some of the gems include the large, easy-to-grow shrub, *Cercis canadensis* 'Forest Pansy', which has heart-shaped, dark purple leaves that positively glow when planted with sunlight behind them; a purple-black opium poppy, *Papaver somniferum* 'Black Beauty', which is Rococo in its over-the-top, ruffled elegance; a tiny, delicate viola called 'Molly Sanderson', which is about as black a plant as you'll find, and the rather weird-looking *Oxalis triangularis* 'Atropurpurea', which is tender, so you need to bring the corms in for winter. Other great candidates for this garden included the chocolate cosmos, *Cosmos atrosanguineus*, which is luxurious both in its chocolate scent and its deep maroon colour; *Angelica sylvestris* 'Purpurea', a fine, sturdy plant with shiny, plum-coloured buds and flowers and the frost-tender *Canna* 'Wyoming', a very beautiful herbaceous plant with wonderful purple and green foliage and startling orange flowers. Cannas

are very heavy feeders and will appreciate regular liquid feeds that are high in potash, such as tomato feed. As it will disappear completely in winter, a low-growing *Viburnum davidii* was planted beside it to create a mixture of summer and winter interest in the bed. Starring roles also went to *Dahlia* 'Bishop of Llandaff' which has wine-tinged, dark green leaves and velvet-textured, rich red blooms, hot pink-purple *Liatris spicata*, ornamental banana *Musa basjoo* and the black-leaved elder, *Sambucus nigra* 'Gerda' ('Black Beauty').

Other good black options include the much-in-vogue, black-stemmed *Phyllostachys nigra*; the *Ophiopogon planiscapus* 'Nigrescens' which is a grass-like plant that looks wonderful planted in conjunction with *Imperata cylindrica* 'Rubra'; the dark-leaved hazel, *Corylus maxima* 'Purpurea'; the Boston ivy, *Parthenocissus tricuspidata* 'Veitchii', with dark red-purple – almost black – leaves, and the wonderful Grass tree, *Xanthorrhoea australis*, which has a black, charred-looking stem – this is best kept in a pot as it must be brought inside for the winter.

A mixture of Hart's tongue fern, *Asplenium scolopendrium*, hostas and *Fatsia japonica*, planted en masse, swept around to the second courtyard, which was cooler in mood, to contrast with the exotica of the lower beds. Here, a perfectly circular lawn was complemented by *Phormium tenax* Purpureum Group, and the ornamental grasses, mscanthus and stipa, while the lower-growing *Heuchera* 'Palace Purple' was block-planted beneath the cantilevered concrete bench. ■

Opposite: A tropical concoction of chocolate cosmos, banana, canna, fatsia and liatris.

This page: The flowers of *Dahlia* 'Bishop of Llandaff', *Canna* 'Wyoming' and *Angelica sylvestris* 'Purpurea' provide rich bursts of colour amongst the foliage of this dark planting scheme.

Dotty

A gardener who followed trends and fashion had been bitten by the architectural bug and wanted plants that would stand out and add drama to a colourful site.

On some of the *Home Front* gardens, we have clients who have just as strong ideas about the plants that should go in the plot, as they do about the landscaping. Jan was in this category – she had very definite desires for the planting scheme in her new garden.

Having done the cottage garden thing in a previous garden, she had decided to move on to architectural, exotic plants – she was a bit of a trend fanatic, liked to be up to date and was inspired by the new and unusual. This was graphically illustrated by her existing collection of potted plants that had made the move from her previous garden a short distance away. The hints were strong and the Mediterranean/exotic look was clearly going to be the order of the day.

There are a few plants that are must-haves in order to create a hot, exotic look. Central to this scheme was a Chusan palm, *Trachycarpus fortunei*, which gives instant impact and shape with its stunningly architectural foliage. Most of the remaining planting was situated in a border around the new raised lawn that surrounded the sardine-

can edge of the overall design. The deck was laid out in the same shape as the lawn and included sunken water troughs that were mainly planted with flag iris, *Iris pseudacorus*, that had been retrieved from an existing pool in the garden. These were a little out of shape and so they were cut back to encourage strong new growth. A new hedge of bamboos was planted to the side of the deck and along the surrounding island walkways that led to the lawn. A jungle of *Trachycarpus fortunei*, the olive tree *Olea europaea*, phormiums, agapanthus and various grasses were also set beside the walkway, but at a slight depth so they didn't tower above you. A variegated agave, *Agave americana* 'Variegata', became one of the new focal points, its striking foliage standing out in a sea of green. The main idea behind the planting scheme was to soften the hard landscaping and structure and to create a barrier across the garden, dividing the lawn from the deck. Other feature plants included phlox, *Astelia chathamica*, and, of course, one of my favourite exotics, the *Dicksonia antarctica*. ■

Opposite: A view from above reveals the dramatic sunburst patterns of the *Dicksonia antarctica*, iris, phormium, cordyline and the trachycarpus.

Above and right: The brilliant blue of the agapanthus flowers provides a splash of colour amongst the green leafy foliage of the bamboos, palms and the existing irises – which were pruned back to give them a new lease of life.

Ramped

Carving out a new, modern garden from an older, more traditional one led us to move forward with design but to go back and look to the past for planting inspiration.

This was already a beautiful garden, with existing mature trees and shrubs planted in a traditional English cottage-garden style. There were roses and flowering shrubs planted around the edges and floating beds in the lawn. This was far too old-fashioned and high maintenance for this young family, but I decided to use planting to enhance the original feel of the garden rather than replace it.

A beautiful magnolia had been planted many years ago and was happily established, having developed into an absolutely gorgeous specimen, underplanted with a selection of ferns. We kept this planting and augmented it by adding more ferns and some astrantias. At the back of the garden, there was a glorious wilderness, an area that had, perhaps, been unplanned and planted haphazardly with some lovely specimen shrubs. I wanted to leave most of it, because it provided an invisible maintenance area behind some secret passageways.

We planted specimen, feathered silver birch, *Betula pendula*, to add an architectural feel – these trees are the perfect size for small gardens and they seldom get out of control. The trees demonstrated another use of planting, as they provided screening from the neighbours so that they didn't have to view the large, imposing structure of the architectural cubes, which functioned as a garden office. Bold plantings of birches around the cubes softened its strong shape and ferns planted underneath melted them into the rest of the garden.

The silver theme of the planting was continued throughout the garden and was used to accentuate the stainless steel and slate of the cube office: the silver-trunked birches brought a great deal of elegance and movement. In the herbaceous border, there was *Stachys byzantina* with silvery, furry foliage, the silver-variegated *Euonymus* and *Sedum spectabile*, with its succulent, cool blue-green leaves and sturdy, eye-catching stems. The blue-grey hostas with broad-veined leaves were almost the same shade as the slate of the office building. The Japanese painted fern, *Athyrium niponicum* var. *pictum*, was also planted for its delicately marked fronds, which have a metallic sheen.

These silvers and other foliage and flower colours contrasted with the green simplicity of the lawn that made up most of the central part of the garden. Foliage shades came from geraniums with evergreen leaves that redden as they age, *Ligularia* with large, purple-tinged leaves and the rich green fronds of ferns such as the crested hart's tongue fern, *Asplenium scolopendrium* 'Cristatum', *Cyrtomium fortunei* and the soft shield fern, *Polystichum setiferum*.

Against the silver and green foliage, flamboyant flower colours formed accents around the garden, including the vibrant egg-yolk yellow of the ligularias' daisy flowers, the pale and rich pink plumes of astilbes, the long-lasting, magenta heads of *Achillea millefolium* 'Cerise Queen', and the paler, salmon-pink *Achillea* 'Salmon Beauty'. The yellow plumes of *Solidago* and bright pink flowerheads of the sedums continued a theme of pink and gold. The *Sorbus* burst through the deck and made a striking specimen plant with its rich crop of red berries.

All these were planted to keep the garden looking colourful and textural over the summer months but, in winter, it would have quite a different feel as the herbaceous plants would die back to reveal the bare bones of the garden. The winter focus would be on the shape and form of the horseshoe turf slope, the cube and the skeletal, pale trunks of the birches and the aged magnolia. It will look superb on a misty, frosty morning. ∎

Opposite: A selection of ferns, astilbes and achilleas will take over this shady area.

Below left to right: This garden was planted with a silver theme, but we added accents throughout the beds using colourful foliage and flowers, such as lush green ferns, the magenta *Achillea millefolium* 'Cerise Queen' and the bright yellow ligularias.

Igloo

A science fiction, space-age design called for the planting of dramatic architectural specimens which would not have looked out of place on a Los Angeles movie set.

The planting in this garden was a massively important part of the design as the plants needed to match the theatricality created by the surreal white concrete structures that were reminiscent of a 1970s James Bond movie set. I wanted to create a jungle effect that had to be crawled through, so I went to the Tropics biome at the Eden project, in Cornwall, to see the palms and get inspiration from them. Palms seemed the perfect choice, since their arching fronds would give the dramatic effect I wanted. The Chusan palm, *Trachycarpus fortunei*, is one of the hardiest palms available to grow in the UK, so I used several of these as the drama queens of the garden.

A medium-sized shrub, *Euonymus japonicus*, was planted at the base of the palms as ground cover and to mask the tunnel entrance that would bring the kids into their igloo. There were plantings of evergreen *Fatsia japonica*, with its extremely tropical-looking leaves, and

swathes of sedums and *Hebe* 'Red Edge' all around the sunken seating area, softening the look of the concrete. The slightly hairy-looking, vivid pink-purple flowers of *Liatris spicata* provided startling colour contrast against the white concrete. The advantage of planting evergreens against the white concrete is that they provide all-year colour and prevent the landscaping looking cold and harsh in the winter without the benefit of sunlight.

As I have mentioned, to achieve the different, out-of-this-world feel for this garden, I had to use striking plants, which meant gathering a collection of plants that had originated from all around the world. I used a really large specimen of *Eucalyptus parviflora* from Australia. Eucalyptus is an excellent tree in a small garden because it looks great as an ornamental and you can keep it fairly small by cutting it back quite harshly. Don't worry, eucalyptus has a natural

tendency to regenerate – if it has been environmentally damaged in the wild, it will just sprout back with lovely green juvenile leaves that turn grey-green as they mature. We also included a few scary plants, too, such as *Dicksonia squarrosa*, that remind you of a movie set – or when Dr Who comes out of his Tardis onto a strange planet! This dicksonia is a little bit different from my old favourite tree fern, *Dicksonia antarctica*, as its stems are more slender and it has a distinctive whitish underside to the fronds. Planting cannas, bamboos and grasses also contributed to the crowded, steamy jungle feel.

Large specimens of winged spindle, *Euonymus alatus* and the smoke bush, *Cotinus* 'Grace', were also planted, both of which will give spectacular colour in autumn. The euonymus, when it has lost its leaves in winter, reveals stems with fascinating corky wings giving them the appearance of being square in shape. ■

Opposite: Using large, exotic specimens helps to create a crowded, overgrown jungle effect.

Above left to right: The leaves of a *Euonymus japonicus* cast a wonderful shadow on the white concrete structures, while the purple flowerheads of the *Liatris spicata* and miscanthus bring colour and contrast to the garden when set against the landscaping.

Trad Mod

Relaxed curves were the order of the day for the plan in a garden where the planting was to be delightfully traditional with room for a vegetable plot.

The design idea for this garden was based on the landscape designer Humphrey Repton's picturesque ideas of a fully planted, curvaceous landscape in which the curves led you round to different focal points in the garden. This large, suburban garden, well-surrounded on all sides by trees and tall hedging, was split by a large, serpentine lawn that created generous-sized planting areas, and, as you followed the lawn around the garden, large specimen trees and shrubs appeared as focal points. We used deciduous trees such as a feathered Himalayan birch *Betula utilis* var. *jacquemontii*, with its beautiful white bark, the flame-like *Carpinus betulus* 'Fastigiata', and *Liquidambar styraciflua*, which is suitable for moist but well-drained sites and has beautiful autumn colouring. For smaller spaces, you could choose a feathered *Cornus kousa*, with its huge white bracts in early summer, or the Judas tree, *Cercis siliquastrum*, which has a quirky little habit of producing pretty pink, pea-like flowers that grow directly from the bark on the branches before the new leaves unfurl. As an alternative

to the contorted hazel, *Corylus avellana* 'Contorta', the contorted willow, *Salix babylonica* var. *pekinensis* 'Tortuosa' is a great choice for wet soils and can also be hacked severely to keep a check on its size. For a really tiny tree as a good focal point at the front of a bed, I planted a *Prunus persica* 'Nana', an ornamental peach, which has branches of wall-to-wall pink flowers in spring and will even produce fruit.

We incorporated some evergreen plants for winter form by using the fast growing *Eucalyptus gunnii*, the strawberry tree, *Arbutus unedo*, which is a wonderful tree that has the curious habit of producing its fruit and flowers at the same time, and a couple of large *Thuja* specimens which acted as permanent punctuations in the beds. A large specimen of *Cornus controversa* 'Variegata' became a light-coloured focal point near the back of the garden and a large-sized, flowering mahonia made a bright yellow splash.

The planting was mixed and diverse as the conditions varied from wet and shady to dry and sunny. Grasses

were planted in the drier areas of the garden, including calamagrostis, with its erect plumes, the tall-flowered miscanthus and even taller cortaderias, offset by smaller carex with a neat habit of growth. For interest and variation, there were intermittent plantings of sea hollies (*Eryngium* species) and cardoon, *Cynara cardunculus*, with their prickly, thistle-like appearance; the large, tropical-leaved banana, *Musa basjoo*; the very tactile purple sage, *Salvia officinalis* 'Purpurascens', phormiums, cordylines and the cool, silver-grey foliaged *Santolina chamaecyparissus*.

For the wetter areas, there were large swathes of *Gunnera manicata*, with its enormous, prehistoric-looking leaves, pink feathery-plumed astilbes and white-flowered zantedeschias. In more shady areas, there were ferns and *Geranium macrorrhizum* – which is an extremely good, ground-covering plant in areas where growing conditions are difficult.

For a quirky touch, a raised, stainless-steel-edged bed had an area planted with cabbages. ■

Opposite: The lawn swings down in vast curves, passing undulating, heavily planted beds and beautiful specimen trees.

Below left to right: Drifts of grasses such as miscanthus and *Pennisetum setaceum* bring a soft, relaxed feel to the beds, while the *Liquidambar styraciflua* provides a wonderful, vibrant burst of autumn colour in the garden.

To the waters and the wild
Follow the yellow brick road – a meandering path wound its way through a magical woodland to create a family garden and a plant-lover's haven.

This was an average suburban garden with a 22m (75ft) lawn and a single border of shrubs along one side, massively overlooked by the gable end of a neighbouring house at the bottom. The children were the only family members using the garden, but the owners wanted this to be a place were the whole family could hang out. A winding, meandering path surrounded by plants, chosen for their foliage colours and form, led to a pond planted with rushes and sedges – more greenery discreetly hid the fence, which was positioned around the pond to make it safe for the children.

The planting throughout was in layers with tall specimen trees of whitebeam, *Sorbus aria*, and Himalayan birch, *Betula utilis* var. *jacquemontii*, used as screening at the end of the garden. All this layered planting gave the whole garden a woodland feeling and a sense of privacy for the first time. These trees also did much more than simply act as a screen; they were carefully selected so that in autumn their foliage would change colour to yellows and reds before finally dropping off in winter, completely changing the look again. A mature specimen of winged spindle, *Euonymus alatus*, was very prominently planted, providing a pivotal splash of crimson in autumn. Deciduous trees are a really easy way to introduce drama in any garden because of their transformations through the seasons; from bare branches in winter to bright green, new leafy growth in spring through to the darker adult foliage in summer and then the autumn colour changes bringing a vibrant palette of yellows, oranges, pinks, reds and browns. Nowhere is this better illustrated than in the woodlands and forests of New England in the United States, an area with which the client had close family connections, which lent a nostalgic feel to the garden.

But it's not only the dying foliage of autumn that provides interesting foliage colours in a garden; many plants are naturally colourful while in leaf. There is the foliage of the purple-leaved forms of *Cotinus coggygria* and *Berberis thunbergii* f. *atropurpurea*; the magnificent reds of some of the Japanese maples (*Acer palmatum*); the cool, silvery shades of evergreen lavenders and santolinas and even the jet black foliage of the grass-like *Ophiopogon planiscapus* 'Nigrescens'.

A lower layer of younger and smaller trees and shrubs all gave the garden a much-needed feeling of anticipation and mystery, since you could no longer see what was in front of you as the pathway wound its way down the garden. Hazels, (*Corylus*) with their distinctive, large, rounded leaves and the evergreen, red-tinged foliage of photinias, with bright red new growth, were dotted through the garden. *Rhus typhina* 'Dissecta', which throws out spreading limbs of long, deeply dissected, drooping leaves, gives amazing autumn colour, and when the leaves finally fall off, you're left with the dark pink, furry, conical flowers at the branch tips.

Large trees can be used closer to buildings to give more interesting views from windows, particularly if they have good foliage shape, habit or colour; they give a building more of a tie to the garden. For this garden, we looked out of the windows and checked that the views from the inside out were all interesting and effective. White-barked birches and yellow-foliaged *Gleditsia triacanthos* 'Sunburst' were situated near them for maximum viewing.

As in all woodlands, there was a low understorey of planting. Here it included *Caryopteris* x *clandonensis* 'Worcester Gold', with its golden foliage and blue flowers, alongside fluffy potentillas and hardy geraniums. Here and there were pockets of mass-planted variegated irises, (*Iris pallida* 'Variegata') with their bold green and white, sword-shaped leaves. Mass plantings of sedums near the house, and ferns throughout the whole garden, gave a cohesive vein throughout the beds. ■

Opposite: A sylvan setting with large boulders that function as focal points and seats.

Right from top: *Cotinus coggygria* and *Euonymus alatus* create strong, dark splashes of colour through the trees, and the cotinus also provides a wonderful backdrop for the brighter, yellow foliage of *Gleditsia triacanthos* 'Sunburst'.

High gloss

In a sleek, city space that needed to be an entertaining area as well as a garden, soft plants were the perfect accessories to add colour, contrast and texture.

The secret behind the planting in this garden was to be creating level changes to soften and blend the many background materials. Plants were used to link different colours, textures and materials into one cohesive unit. The initial problem with the garden was one of an awkward site divided. The plant material related to and reacted to first of all its man-made background and then of course to have a relationship with its neighbouring plant.

The style of planting was slightly architectural –a soft modern take on a chic courtyard garden. In relatively recent times we have two periods of fashion for architectural plants, plants with striking forms, be that in overall shape or dramatic stems or foliage. This was during the early seventies and the late nineties. But what you discover is that to achieve real contrast in a planting scheme, don't be too blunt with your architectural features. A new style creeping in is using the best of two worlds – strong statements softened by more traditional planting of herbaceous perennials. So to achieve a dramatic yet soft look which can include lots of passion, bed your statements into a sea of delightful accompaniments such as alchemilla, heuchera, and hardy geraniums. Here, the architectural shape of the broad leaves of *Hosta fortunei* var. *hyacinthina* were used in contrast with the softer outline of the nepeta, while the bold leaves of *Rheum palmatum* were complemented by

Geranium himalayense 'Gravetye'. Colour was also contrasted with a bottom layer of blue separated from a top line of predominantly yellow plants – *Achillea* 'Moonshine' and *Ilex crenata* 'Golden gem'.

A Japanese maple, *Acer palmatum* 'Burgundy Lace' was used starkly against a wooden-clad wall containing a circular white opening that highlights the delicate cuts in the leaves. Standing one plant out on its own, using it as a specimen causes you to examine its inherent beauty. This was underplanted by *Euonymus* 'Emerald 'n' Gold', providing an rich colour contrast.

A feature of planting a garden that contains raised beds is to plant at ground level at the base of the lowest raised bed which melts all the structure in to the ground, cushions the blow of using hard materials and softens the appearance of the garden by creating a fountain of foliage that seems to drip from layer to layer. Raised beds can look very drab in winter so it's a good idea to include a good deal of evergreen material. Here we included *Osmanthus heterophyllus*, an invaluable plant for its glossy holly-like leaves and superbly fragrant flowers in autumn, blue fescue (*Festuca glauca* 'Elijah Blue') and a dwarf mountain pine (*Pinus mugo pumilio*). Continuity of interest in flowering is catered for from the early flowering dicentras (*Dicentra spectabilis*), through summer-flowering Daylilies (*Hemerocallis*) through to the late summer-/early autumn-flowering cimicifuga. ∎

Opposite: The black mosaic tiles beautifully set off the different foliage forms and colours of the hostas and nepetas and provide year-round colour throughout the garden.

Left top and bottom: The delicate yet dramatic purple leaves of the *Acer palmatum* 'Burgundy Lace' are shown off to great effect by the projection screen behind, while the glossy green leaves of *Heuchera cylindrica* 'Greenfinch' spill over out of their beds, softening the decking.

Rapunzel

In this garden, romantic and English cottage style planting were the perfect combination to create a gentle, fragrant fairytale garden.

The cottage garden planting style remains a perennial favourite. Of course, it has evolved from much grittier roots; it was once more of a functional vegetable plot with flowers that was attached to a worker's cottage than the chocolate box image we associate with cottage gardens today. But it is that idealized picture of romantic arbours, traditional roses and a profusion of blooms that formed the inspiration for this seaside garden. This sort of planting is all about sunshine and colour and is the type of planting that you can totally relax into and just enjoy – there's nothing threatening or challenging about it – it just looks pretty and soft.

In this garden, we used the archetypal cottage-garden plant, the rose. The arbours and trellises were covered in roses that look traditional, but that flower almost continuously – many of the old garden roses bloom only once. *Rosa* Agatha Christie is a modern, large-flowered climber with beautiful fragrant, glowing pink flowers, it's repeat flowering and is great for walls and pillars. *R*. High Hopes is also a modern, large-flowered climber with light rose-pink, double flowers that keep going until autumn and it's moderately scented. The fairytale tower was also softened at the base by climbers, and shrub roses such as *R*. Eglantyne.

The rest of the garden was filled with lots and lots of big, blousy, colourful plants. *Lavatera* x *clementii* 'Rosea' added a soft, billowy cloud of pink to the garden and provided a good colour contrast with the lavender, *Lavandula angustifolia,* planted beside it. The double

flowered *Kerria japonica* 'Pleniflora' added essential early spring colour and *Abelia* x *grandiflora* is an evergreen shrub that goes on flowering forever. Planting herbs, such as rosemary, *Rosmarinus officinalis*, near the seating area and doorways, means that the plants can release their scent as you brush by them to add a wonderful fragrance to frequently used areas.

Against the wall we planted *Cercis canadensis* 'Forest Pansy' and underplanted with artemisia; this combination created an eye-catching contrast between the gracefully arching, purple-leaved branches of the cercis and the cool silvery mound of the artemisia. Yellow-flowered day lilies (*Hemerocallis*), planted through the beds, provided flowers whose beauty lasts but a day but they are produced in a long succession, and the *Hibiscus syriacus* 'Oiseau Bleu' is another quintessential part of the English cottage-garden style. White Japanese anemones, such as *Anemone* x *hybrida* 'Honorine Jobert', are one of the lowest maintenance herbaceous plants available, they will grow in quite deep shade, require no staking and also make a good choice for late summer and early autumn flowers when so many other plants have finished. *Achillea* Summer Pastels Group has to be one of the longest flowering cottage-style plants and comes in mouth-watering, ice-cream colours. In contrast to the texture and colours of much of the other traditional, soft planting, the sea hollies, (*Eryngium* species) with their thistle-like, silvery foliage, added tall punctuation marks dotted through the beds.

There are so many suitable plants for the cottage garden that it really does come down to personal choice and to what you can successfully fit into your borders! A few favourites worth mentioning are clematis, hardy geraniums, lamb's ears (*Stachys byzantina*), violas, catmint (*Nepeta*), baptisias, alstromerias, poppies (*Papaver orientale* and *P. somniferum*), monkshood (*Aconitum*), lupins and peonies – but the possibilities and combinations are endless! ■

Opposite: A tranquil setting for breakfast, surrounded by aromatic plants and a relaxing cottage garden.

Above left to right: Lovely, romantic lavatera. Take cuttings as this is great as a juvenile but it doesn't grow old gracefully. Lavatera is a beautiful cottage garden plant and was happily placed with rosemary, hibiscus and day lilies in an colourful, fragrant combination that reflected the romantic mood of the garden.

Nouveau gardening

Arranging planting on many different levels so that a variety of specimens cascade over raised beds, lent a softness and drama to a stylish, architectural design.

The style of this garden was dictated to me by the client's love of the Art Nouveau period, a style that evolved in Europe during the last two decades of the nineteenth century and the beginning of the twentieth. My interpretation of this style for the overall design was that the scheme had to be elegantly flamboyant, slightly melancholic and rich in colour. I needed to create a garden that had to live up to the style in terms of both structure and plants.

The site sloped heavily down towards the house which made it a difficult site in many ways, but one that also gave views from the windows that would allow the plants to be appreciated at different levels. The interpretation of this style through plants was a very personal one and was influenced by a visit to the Horta Museum in Brussels, and through the appreciation of Aubrey Beardsley's sensational illustrations for Oscar Wilde's *Salome* in 1894. Something graphic, architectural and theatrical needed to have its feet in a cloud of softness, and so the planting scheme was based on the interpretation – my interpretation – of an existing design style.

To create an elegant, simple planting scheme, I limited my palette of plants to a relatively small number of species. They were divided into startling specimens, luxurious ground covers and star performers, but all were selected for the purpose of covering the ground in the beds with vigorous shrubs that would allow groups of colours to burst through. The colours chosen were predominantly white, lilac, purples and pinks to complement the rich aubergine shade in which the architecture had been painted.

Creating strong boundaries from hard materials, such as walls and fences, would have segregated the garden from the existing landscape of terraced gardens. Rather than separate it so harshly, a more delicate effect was achieved by planting slender trees such as a multi-stemmed birch, the silk tree, *Albizia julibrissin*, and a glorious southern catalpa, *Catalpa bignonioides*. Two pencil-thin Italian cypress, *Cupressus sempervirens*, were planted in white ceramic pots to enhance the semi-enclosed courtyard. Tumbling down the slopes on either side, at the base of the trees were *Hydrangea macrophylla maculata*, *Verbena*

bonariensis, *Fatsia japonica*, *Salvia officinalis*, *Hemerocallis* 'Pink Damask' and *Achillea* 'Lilac Queen'. Art Nouveau pots were filled with *Tulbaghia violacea* and a dazzling selection of purple cordylines were used to bring a strong wine colour to the lower beds. The scheme was intended to be luxurious and romantic, but it was also one that did not need a huge amount of maintenance.

Symmetry was the blueprint, and to ensure that the garden would appear to be a series of mirror images, the main specimens were bought in pairs. Thus a set of *Aralia elata* created the appearance of an archway as a visitor stepped through sections of a circular raised bed. The thorny stems, exotic foliage and panicles of flowers looked dramatic against the vision of what was to come, but also softened the view back to the house. Other feature plants in this part of the garden included half standard *Hydrangea paniculata* 'Grandiflora' with their glorious blooms of drooping white flowers suggesting a fountain. Underplanted with golden hostas, they created a startling combination. The top level had semi-standard rosemary planted in a bed of soft-hued lavenders. ∎

Opposite: Plants cascade symmetrically down the terrace to the specimen *Hydrangea paniculata* 'Grandiflora' dripping with white blooms.

Below left to right: To add to the lush planting of the beds, pots were placed around the garden and planted up with lavender, *Hydrangea paniculata* 'Grandiflora' – whose flowers seem to fall into the pool of hostas planted beneath them – and *Tulbaghia violacea*.

Case study
Meteor

It is always interesting to visit a garden in winter, as you get a completely different impression of the space. My initial visit to this garden was late in the year, but even then, with many of the plants having died back, it was obvious that it had been carefully tended at one time and the long, narrow strip had been well planted by a previous owner. Small garden trees, such as *Robinia pseudoacacia* 'Frisia' and birches, hugged the boundaries and a mixture of herbaceous perennials and suburban shrubs, such as *Choisya ternata*, filled the narrow borders. Despite its awkward shape, it was a lovely garden. Subsequent visits in the spring revealed it as a most enchanting space and even raised the question as to whether we should be working there at all! Unplanned gardens, places that have evolved within the tradition of old-fashioned planting styles and have then subsequently relaxed and done their own thing for a few years can have a beautiful, wistful feel. But if they don't meet the needs of the new owners, they are not working in the required way, which, here, needed to be an exciting and relaxing place for a modern family to enjoy.

Case study
Meteor

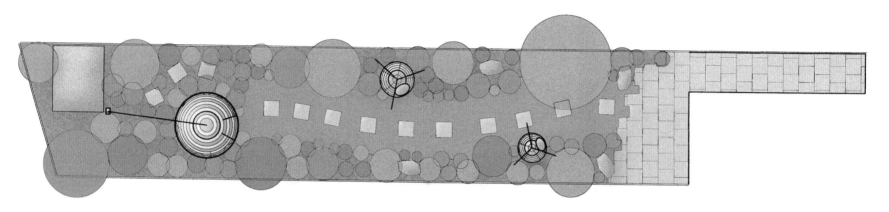

Above: The trick here was carving out a new garden from an old one and the design was very simple – we just added some new structures, including a room and some seating, to an old garden and replanted the whole site. A simple stone patio leads to a stepping stone pathway which leads the visitor through the garden and to the many surprises in store.

Jackie and Howard, our clients, are a very modern couple with a small child; they both work in the creative side of advertising. They wanted me to interpret their love of nature, their appreciation of colour, mood and the excitement of good design into their plot to create a garden that would suit their needs as a family. They wanted the garden to incorporate their awareness of the sky and wanted to open up the possibilities of framing views; they loved the existing dense planting and wanted to enhance the romantic style, not to subdue it with imported alien visions. They needed a hard surface that would work as an outside dining area and wanted space for seating throughout the garden. Most of all, an outdoor office space with a difference was required – from now on Jackie would be working from home and where better to set up her desk than in her inspirational garden?

Design and materials

The design evolved over a long period of time and after many visits to the site. To reflect the romantic, fairyland feel that the owners wanted, I decided on a very simple curved shape that would be realized in a stepping stone pathway meandering through the long, narrow space. Near the house, a random-stone patio was laid in Indian limestone, which is extremely porous and so had to be sealed. In order

to retain the gentle feel of the garden, this hard landscaping was duly softened by the surrounding ebb and flow of herbs and roses.

Two hanging seats were designed to enable Jackie and Howard to sit in the garden and gently sway, to revolve within their space and to hover lightly above the planting. These seats were inspired by notions of those loft-living, 'easy-like-Sunday-morning', clear-acrylic spheres that seemed to epitomize the free and easy, urban lifestyle of the 1970s. Our versions of this idea were a little more hard-wearing and were constructed by welding curved ribs of steel into spheres. A circular opening was left in each one through which you could clamber in. These seats were hung from a tripod of steel poles, which themselves created strongly architectural, tepee-like forms.

The architectural centrepiece of this particular garden, however, was an extremely difficult piece of engineering to work out and subsequently to manufacture.

When I first met the clients, it had quickly become apparent how important it was to them to have a view of the sky above. They talked about visits to a garden in County Cork, at the very south of Ireland, that you entered through a mound to find yourself at the centre of a crater-like construction with grass mounds forming a continuous wall all around you. This formation

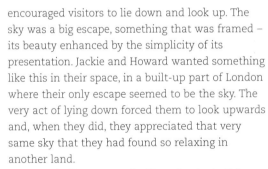

encouraged visitors to lie down and look up. The sky was a big escape, something that was framed – its beauty enhanced by the simplicity of its presentation. Jackie and Howard wanted something like this in their space, in a built-up part of London where their only escape seemed to be the sky. The very act of lying down forced them to look upwards and, when they did, they appreciated that very same sky that they had found so relaxing in another land.

For a similar reason, the ideas for the building which was to be Jackie's home office started out as two hanging baskets, one laid on top of the other to create a sphere with a slice taken off the top to reveal the sky. All around the outside of it would be planted, again, to soften the material and shape of the structure.

Of course, this fanciful structure wouldn't have been waterproof or practical, so the evolution continued with the development of the idea for a simple steel sphere with a lid that winched up to reveal the sky and a door that opened – drawbridge-style – to allow you to enter the football-shaped enclosure. A tiled surface within gave the room a bright feel while also enhancing the idea of a very modern space capsule. Flaps in the steel shell could be pushed open from the inside to reveal twenty plates of coloured glass, so at night, strong lighting beneath a metal grill in

the floor turned the sphere into a giant lantern casting magical, varied colours over the exterior tiles. The whole structure was set in a slight depression in the garden and was underplanted with ferns, so that it felt as if a meteor had landed from outer space and settled in a naturalistic garden.

After the main sphere was put in place, huge boulders were dotted throughout the garden to enhance the natural feel of the garden. They were used as focal points and also doubled up as practical seats. For these we decided to use a stone called Kent ragstone, as its bright colour reflected the light.

Creating the garden

Access into this garden had been a primary concern from the outset as the house was terraced and there was no side access or any possibility of bringing materials and structures through other people's gardens. So, in a military-style operation that had been planned a month before we arrived on site, a crane was hired to lift all of the elements over the top of the house and into the garden at the rear. In order to create a place from which all the site work could be conducted, we had to commandeer the living room of the house. To minimize the damage and mess caused by the build, we panelled the floor, walls and ceiling of this

Above: The garden had some lovely existing plants, so we focused on changing the garden by adding some hard landscaping and structures. Because of their weight and lack of access to the site, the spherical, steel chairs and the steel sphere had to be lifted over the house and into position in the garden by crane. Feet and framework were installed ready for their arrival.

Case study
Meteor

space in wood, in effect, creating a room within a room. The small window at the far end of the living room was then enlarged to create an opening which improved access into the garden for all the materials and machinery needed during the build. After our departure, the couple converted this opening into double doors.

Access is one of the most important considerations when you are attempting large-scale landscaping in any situation. If there is no rear or side access to your garden, as in this situation, you might need to consider hiring a crane to bring in materials, or struggle through the house with them. Be aware that your original design may not be realistic if there is no practical way of bringing in the necessary materials, and if your budget will not stretch to hiring a crane or

suchlike. It was a challenge in this location to ensure that the potential difficulties were overcome. As well as hiring a crane to lift the large and heavy items, we also had to make sure that all our materials would arrive on day four of a fourteen-day build. The local authority had given us a licence to close the road for that day, our crane was hired and our most prominent features – the boulders from the quarry, our steel seats and tripods, the sphere and its mechanical components, along with our feature tree – had to arrive in ordered succession.

Planting

The plans for the planting in this garden had to take into consideration and maintain its existing relaxed feel and also needed to enhance its romantic ambience, rather than to contrast with or work against it. It's important to appreciate that this atmosphere already existed within the garden, and it derived, in large part, from the use of garden plants that were not predominantly native British species. This would be the way we would continue. Naturalistic visions of native wildflower meadows are romantically beautiful, but they do take a lot of planning and maintenance and would definitely have felt contrived in this situation. So the gentle romantic feel was achieved by using relaxed planting which would, it must be said, also mean

relaxed maintenance; this garden was not about being kept trim and neat.

Our number one plant was a sweet gum, *Liquidambar styraciflua* – I used a mature specimen to create impact and to help divide the garden as well as provide a woodland feel to the planting. This tree has wonderful maple-like leaves which give spectacular colour in the autumn, turning from green to orange, red and purple. It was planted next to our sphere and the combination of the two created a narrow passageway that successfully divided the space and encouraged you to go on deeper into the garden. We introduced other trees to the garden too, including a silver birch, *Betula pendula* which is an excellent tree for small gardens, an Antarctic beech, *Nothofagus antarctica* – again for its stunning, glossy green foliage which turns yellow in autumn and a small, but beautiful, evergreen tree *Acacia dealbata,* which would provide colour and texture throughout the winter with its fern-like, hairy leaves and fragrant, yellow flowers.

In order to hide an unsightly shed which would have detracted from the natural scheme, we planted a hazel, *Corylus avellana,* in front of it. A host of pink patio roses were planted outside the back door in full sun, as Jackie wanted some colour in the garden. These were low, almost ground hugging and, when in full flower, created an explosion of vivid pink.

Case study
Meteor

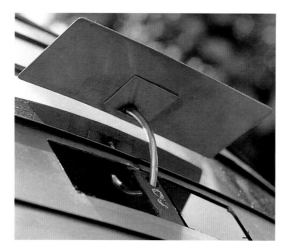

Above: Simple, stainless steel hatches could be opened from the inside to transform our structure from a sleek sphere to a multi-coloured lantern. To soften the impact of the sphere by day, it was set amongst a bed of lush, green ferns.

Opposite: The overall design was based on the relationship of shapes, with one spherical form working against another, but always surrounded by arching and overhanging trees and bedded in by shrubby planting.

The side boundaries of this garden already held a mixture of shrubs that left no room for any climbing plants, but the legs of the tripods played perfect host to rampant climbing plants such as clematis, the golden hop, *Humulus lupulus* 'Aureus', and *Fallopia baldshuanica*. In the shade of the larger shrubs, geraniums, foxgloves and ferns worked wonders and added to the cottagey, woodland feel. Laying out defined borders was not appropriate to this relaxed and romantic design and would have imposed a formality that would have jarred with the magical, gentle atmosphere of the garden. So the planting scheme for this garden actually ended up evolving on site, with ferns also being planted randomly at the base of boulders as well as beneath the sphere. The impact of the sphere was gently softened by the existing robinia, whose branches, laden with dazzling yellow foliage, arched in front of it, embracing it and settling it in so that it looked as if it had always been there. ∎

Left to right: The cap was raised from our ball-like structure by means of a steel shaft in the background. This shaft was connected by a stainless steel cable to the top of the cap so that it could be slowly winched up and down.

Opposite: Sitting inside the hanging seats allowed a great freedom of movement, as you turned around in them each new view was framed by the circular opening.

Selected plant list

Acacia dealbata

(Mimosa) Evergreen tree. Sheltered site in full sun (half-hardy – can withstand temperatures down to 0°C), moderately fertile, neutral to acid soil. H 15–30m (50–100ft), S 6–10m (20–30ft).

Betula pendula

(Silver birch) Deciduous tree. Full sun or light dappled shade, moderately fertile, moist but well-drained soil. H 25m (80ft), S 10m (30ft).

Campanula glomerata 'Superba'

(Clustered bellflower) Herbaceous perennial. Sun/partial shade, fertile, neutral to alkaline, moist but well-drained soil. H 60cm (24in), S indefinite.

Clematis 'Alice Fisk'

Deciduous climber. Full sun, with roots in shade in fertile, humus-rich, well-drained soil. H 2–2.4m (6–8ft), S 1m (3ft).

Corylus avellana

(Hazel) Deciduous tree/shrub. Sun/partial shade, fertile, well-drained soil, ideal for chalky soils. H and S 5m (15ft).

Digitalis grandiflora

(Yellow foxglove) Biennial/Perennial. Partial shade, humus-rich soil, will tolerate almost any soil and situation, except very wet and very dry. H to 1m (3ft), S 45cm (18in).

Fallopia baldshuanica

(Russian vine) Deciduous climber. Full sun/partial shade, poor to moderately fertile, moist but well-drained soil. H and S 12m (40ft).

Geranium x oxonianum 'Claridge Druce'

Evergreen perennial. Full sun/partial shade, in any moderately fertile, well-drained soil. H 45–75cm (18–30in), S 60cm (24in).

Humulus lupulus 'Aureus'

(Golden hop) Herbaceous climber. Sun, moderately fertile, moist but well-drained soil. H and S 6m (20ft).

Lavandula angustifolia

(Lavender) Evergreen shrub. Full sun, moderately fertile, well-drained soil. H 1m (3ft), S 1.2m (4ft).

Liatris spicata

(Gayfeather) Herbaceous perennial. Full sun, reliably moist but well-drained soil. H to 1.5m (5ft), S 45cm (18in).

Liquidambar styraciflua

(Sweetgum) Deciduous tree. Full sun/partial shade, moderately fertile, preferably acid or neutral, moist but well-drained soil. H 25m (80ft), S 12m (40ft).

Nothofagus antarctica

(Antarctic beech) Deciduous tree. Full sun, fertile, moist but well-drained, lime-free (acid) soil. H 15m (50ft), S 10m (30ft).

Osmunda regalis 'Purpurascens'

(Royal fern) Deciduous fern. Light, dappled shade, moist, fertile, humus-rich, preferably acid soil. H and S 1.2m (4ft).

Polypodium vulgare

(Common polypody) Evergreen fern. Full sun or dappled shade, with shelter from cold, dry winds, moderately fertile, humus-rich, gritty or stony,

well-drained soil. H 30cm (12in), S indefinite.

Polystichum setiferum 'Plumosomultilobum'

(Soft shield fern) Evergreen fern. Deep/partial shade, fertile, humus-rich, well-drained soil. H and S 50–70cm (20–28in).

Rosa 'Wiltshire'

Deciduous shrub. Full sun, moderately fertile, humus-rich, moist but well-drained soil. H 60cm (2ft), S 1.2m (4ft).

Spiraea japonica 'Little Princess'

Deciduous shrub. Full sun, fertile, moist but well-drained soil. H 50cm (20in), S 1m (3ft).

Thymus 'Doone Valley'

(Thyme) Evergreen subshrub. Full sun, well-drained neutral to alkaline soil. H 12cm (5in), S 35cm (14in).

Thymus vulgaris 'Silver Posie'

(Garden thyme) Evergreen subshrub. Full sun, well-drained neutral to alkaline soil. H 15–30cm (6–12in), S 30cm (12in).

Trachelospermum jasminoides

(Star jasmine) Evergreen climber. Full sun/partial shade, fertile, well-drained soil, provide shelter from cold, drying winds. H 9m (28ft).

Levels

Levels

Changes in level occur in a garden naturally or can be incorporated into a design for practical or aesthetic reasons. Different levels throughout a space simply mean that areas of the garden are at different heights. In Japan, for example, most gardening, by necessity, takes place between the base of steep mountains and the sea, and in the grand Italian gardens, terracing was designed to create usable areas at different levels that were linked together by steps. Drawing on these observations, we can appreciate how changes in level occur naturally in gardens, and see how whole design principles have evolved from the natural topography.

A landscape that is flat can be visually boring and unadventurous and the same is true in gardens; there are no opportunities to hide surprises beneath drops in level and little potential to create vistas beyond slopes. While we may inherit what appears to be difficult terrain, and despair of gardens that slope down to, or away from our property, much intrigue can be created in these situations by thoughtful planning.

Changes in levels equate with drama. They add interest to an otherwise uninspiring location and can be developed into a sympathetic surrounding for a property and create a host of fascinating niches for plants. Visual tricks can be played with scale and aspect to create interesting views, and slopes or terraces can create novel aspects for viewing planting schemes that could not otherwise be considered. When a plant is growing at a level that is below or above the usual line of vision, the view of it changes and you may get to appreciate its overall shape, stem, trunk, foliage or flowers from a previously unconsidered angle. When you move from one specimen to a whole planting scheme, these vistas can be exciting or even intoxicating. Viewing anything in an unexpected way creates inherent interest and when the objects of your attention are living species in a constant state of transition through the seasons, you may be treated to the best seats in the house.

Exploiting potential

Slopes or levels can create excitement by offering potential for a sense of movement throughout a site, both for people and materials. The opportunity to create moving watercourses, interesting pathways and singular focal points stimulates the creative process. And often, a seemingly inhospitable site can yield magical results with opportune planting.

Even gentle changes of level – the most usual situation people experience in the domestic garden – can guide the design of a plot. Getting to know your site and understanding the advantages presented by different natural levels is very important. As you explore an undulating garden, you often find areas that open up to offer spectacular views of landscapes beyond. A raised part of the garden may also be the last place the rays of the setting sun touch in the evening and it could offer the perfect spot to take tea. The benefits of such sites should be exploited. If you have an area that offers a distant view of a church spire surrounded by yew trees, for example, rather than planting a detailed mixed border in front of it, which would draw attention away from the view, consider the creation of a small paved area with seating to enhance your enjoyment of the vista and surround yourself with detailed planting at closer quarters.

Practicalities

On a practical level, the most important considerations are the retention of materials on steep inclines, the drainage of surface water, the choice of plant material and the logistics of their maintenance.

An assessment of the firmness and stability of terrain is essential, especially in the context of turbulent weather conditions that can undermine and erode an unstable slope. Any retaining walls, terracing, pathways or other structures should be built on firm and permanent foundations. This may be the most testing part of the construction process and may involve the use of specialist technical expertise, for example, if you need to introduce structural piles into a site to create deeply embedded foundations.

Drainage should always be considered as a matter of primary concern. It's far better to determine exactly the course of water running down a slope rather than leaving it to chance – it has serious implications with regard to creating a risk of flooding. Drainage also has implications in terms of choice and placement of different types of planting. Moisture-demanding plants and bog plants, for example, are more likely to be successful if planted at the base of a slope where water is most likely to gather; they seldom thrive on a slope where water and nutrients leach straight through the surrounding soil or even run off the top. Conversely, planting an incline with a good mix of trees and shrubs can be a successful way of creating intrigue, but also has practical benefits. The plant roots will bind together the surface soil and help prevent erosion. Think about which plants will offer the greatest benefit in any given site, but don't forget to consider the amount of maintenance they need – and how you will achieve it – to keep them looking good and doing their job. ■

Nouveau gardening

Life can be difficult when you are gardening on a slope. The best way to approach the problem is to celebrate it, to camp it up and to be overly dramatic.

Sometimes drama is the order of the day. When a garden is on a steep incline within a relatively small area – as this one was – there are no two ways of achieving the perfect result. Steps have to be created – lots of them – and the best way to incorporate them into a design is to create a series of terraces which they can link together. Take time to observe the relationship between your garden and your home when you are planning your design, especially from your main viewing areas inside and outside, and try to look at it as a cohesive unit. Think about how you can create a bit of theatre on your site as well as making it one that works both practically and aesthetically.
A garden on a simple slope may look dramatic, but most likely it will be a frustrating site and not rewarding in terms of its use, but a combination of steps and terraces can be the ideal solution.

This garden drew inspiration from gardens such as the Villa Gazoni, near Florence, and added a bit of flamboyant, Busby Berkeley style and a lot of romance through its planting (see Planting, p.106). We drew the idea of a symmetrical route through it from the lines of

ornate Italianate gardens and gave the steps a central role in the story, creating mirror images in both the construction and the planting on either side. It was easy to incorporate the steps into the design, as we needed to maximize the potential to create usable areas on the otherwise impractical slope by levelling off the sloping surfaces to form terraces.

The house was itself set on a different level from the garden so that when you exited it you accessed the garden by walking down steps from the kitchen. The journey through the site then began on a ground-level pathway that traversed a circular raised bed which was laid out over three levels. This opened out into a gently sloping lawn area flanked by white slate pathways and planting, and led to the crowning glory of the garden – a double staircase that enclosed a small paved area fronting onto a simple gated opening.

The journey to the top of the steps revealed a slightly curving wall, which hid the day-to-day practicalities of the garden, namely a large and rather unglamorous shed. The ornate railings which were made in the Art

Nouveau style encouraged the viewer to lean over, absorb the view below and then lift the eyes to the outside world.

Although the garden was built on many different levels which broke up the site and the rather difficult slope, it was also important that we retained a sense of continuity throughout the garden. One way in which this can be achieved is by introducing a common theme to a design, be it through planting, materials or colour. Here, we decided that following one distinct colour through the garden would successfully provide a link between all the different areas. So we used rendered block and concrete as the main construction material for the raised beds and levels and by doing so this allowed us to paint the render and thus introduce one unifying colour throughout the garden. We decided on a deep aubergine colour, which formed a very vibrant and rich backdrop to all the planting. The constantly changing play of light upon it, as it struck the many different angles in this multi-tiered, structural garden, really brought it to life. ■

Opposite: A symphony of plants drip down a tiered garden – three main areas make up the usable space on this hillside garden.

Below left to right: Looking down the garden from the top sweeping staircases lead to specimen cypress trees planted in tall, thin pots. From the bottom up, centred steps framed by hydrangeas, lavenders and aralias lead the eye up.

Hovercraft

An inhospitable sloping site, where gardening is impossible, is transformed by the construction of three pods of decking, yacht rails and planting.

When modernity is called for, fun can be had. Grasping the opportunities that this sloping site presented – and combining an eclectic use of materials with equally eclectic inspirations – resulted in a truly modern creation for this garden.

However, one important consideration when creating an ultra-modern garden on a sloping site, especially in a built-up area, is the effect that your proposed architecture may have on neighbouring gardens. The potential to completely wall or fence your land to a height of 2m (6ft) or more may not exist, and such situations may include places where your planting and structures are visible to a large number of people from some distance away. So do consider the wider landscape before you devise dominant landmarks. It may be more desirable to build into your land, to nestle into the hollows, rather than to create elaborate and obtrusive lookout posts.

Here, however, the contemporary solution we decided on was to create elegant, light terraces on different levels using the material of choice of recent times – decking. The problem with decking – or rather my problem with using decking in this scheme – is that it is most often used only in square, rectangular configurations. The main reason for this is that wood doesn't curve easily. But I find the idea of a curved decking platform stimulating and felt that wood was a material that could live up to the sense of excitement that was inherent in this sloping site. It had exactly the right texture and contemporary feel, and offered practical advantages too. Wood can provide a carefree surface with a durability comparable with harder materials; it is sufficiently lightweight to transport through difficult terrain; it is relatively cheap and fast to build with, and gives striking results in a relatively short space of time. And in combination with other materials,

wood is a lot more flexible than it is given credit for – used here with stainless steel, it allowed me to introduce the desired curves into the construction.

My choice of flooring material for this site was heavy wood in the form of reclaimed oak railway sleepers. Because the terrain was potentially unstable, deep foundations were needed. The site was piled; in effect, table legs made from steel tubes were hammered into the ground to the depth of 7m (22ft). These were then filled with concrete and metal frames mounted on top to create strong surfaces on which to lay the timber. Most of the foundations were invisible. The existing levels of the underlying land were retained and terraces were built above them. Already this created a sense of adventure. The oval shapes of the three main levels gave a truly modern feel to the construction. They were set at different angles to each other and linked by a series of walkways and steps, to make the most of a series of different views. Stainless steel hand rails, inspired by those seen on yachts, leaned out from each terrace – to provide protection and to increase that sense of adventure. A lip of sheet stainless steel was used to clad the base of the railway sleepers and to create a sleek, unified finish. The decks each had their own personalities; one would be a play area for the children, another a dining area, and the third was intended primarily as a host for planting.

The planting (see Planting, p.88) enveloped the construction. On the decks, we planted in containers and in the ground, so that plants emerged through oval openings in the deck; the planting of the surrounding slopes could be enjoyed from the elevated vantage point of the decks themselves. The whole layout, suspended on its slender steel supports, gave the impression of being on an oilrig or on a space ship, as it hovered above the site. ∎

Opposite: Taking inspiration from oil rigs, steel feet were banged into the ground, filled with concrete and used as table legs for oval-shaped terraces which appear to hover above each other.

Below: A succession of ramped walkways and steps creates adventurous connections from one level to another.

Ramped

A large, traditional garden is divided into separate zones to blend modernity and tradition together to create a practical, more manageable space.

Even if you do not suffer the inconvenience of a sloping site and your garden is more or less flat with no changes of level, it can still be interesting, if not strictly necessary, to create different heights in order to break up spaces or offer an alternative perspective on things. Level changing is a device that can work in many ways and can be used to create many different effects. When you have a large, flat area of landscape, creating divisions at different levels can be fun, but it can also be almost a matter of necessity in bringing interest to such a site.

Levels, of course, don't have to mean adding height to a scheme, equally effectively you can dig down and build sunken areas which will break up a flat plot. Small sunken areas can provide excellent areas for dining or just sitting and relaxing. And when water features, such as ponds, are excavated and the prospect of removing large amounts of clay and subsoil from your plot is too much to handle, this excess soil can be used to create mounds. If you plan to excavate, take into consideration that the lower you go the wetter the ground is likely to be. In some situations it is advisable to install drains and a sump pump underneath features to avoid your terrace turning into a pond in wet weather.

Changing levels can also allow the presentation of existing planting within a new perspective, some plants might seem taller when placed at a higher level and you will be able to get a view of the plant from underneath it rather than just at eye level. If you are putting in new plants, this is another factor that you need to think about before you decide which plants to buy and where to position them – plants with interesting bark or undersides to their foliage can look spectacular when placed at a higher level as that is most likely the view you will get of them rather than higher branches. Alternatively, the crown of a tree fern or a long drift

of grasses can look wonderful when they are viewed from above.

Just because you are changing a level doesn't mean that the area actually has to be level – gentle undulations in lawns or beds can also work to great effect to break up the line of the plot. In this way, different architectural landforms can be explored and evolved, to create interesting features that will draw the viewer from the house to examine what prompted such land carving. By both digging down and raising the level of the garden, you can even create rooms beneath an undulating landform.

The ramped horseshoe of turf in this garden was used as a dividing device for a large, open plot. I took inspiration for this idea from the undulating lines of the concrete ramps at the penguin enclosure in London Zoo, but also from the more contemporary wooden ramps used by skate boarders. Rather than simply building a wall to divide this space from the garden beyond, or creating a more subtle division with planting, instead we developed a dynamic curved shape which was then built from white-rendered concrete block walls. The 'arms' of this shape embraced a cohesive and secure play area between them and the entire construction was bedded in by a genteel planting of herbaceous perennials that took its cue from the existing style of the garden (see Planting, p.94). The concrete walls divided this area of the garden from the work zone which was created from two cubes – one steel, one clad in slate, which were suspended one above the other – and finally, from a more relaxed, informal and romantic garden at the end.

So in this garden the levels not only created interest in an otherwise dull, flat plot but they also encouraged the visitor to walk through the grounds and discover what was beyond. ■

Opposite: A strip of lawn enclosed between white-rendered retaining walls drops downwards before rising again to create an unconventional enclosure around an island, decked area. Herbaceous planting helps blend the two together.

Left above: Two cubes (one clad in Welsh slate and the other in stainless steel) float over the garden creating a magical outdoor office space, cubist-style.

Left below: The white colour of the rendered wall creates a beautiful stark background for colourful planting.

Upstairs downstairs

An inner city space makes the best use of whatever outdoor level areas are available by transforming different terraces into urban jungle.

City spaces can provide a great opportunity to develop ideas for exciting landscapes. In urban situations like this one, you have to acknowledge what's going on around you and often have to accept the fact that you're on public show too. The world is indeed a bit of a stage and part of the fun in creating outdoor spaces in these circumstances is the potential to observe and be observed. The mundane activities of people rising in the morning, going into shops, getting on buses, going to work and relaxing in the evening can create delightful diversions. If you're lucky enough to live in a location with such views, make the most of them.

Very few gardens can compete with the enjoyment of a landscape on your roof and while gardening on the rooftop – as we did here – offers some of the best opportunities, it also brings with it a few practical restrictions. One of the most important considerations to take into account is the ownership of the roof. Do you have the freehold over the property and therefore the right to create a garden on the roof? But perhaps even more important is to make absolutely sure that the roof can sustain the enormous load that a new garden will inevitably entail. Adapting a site structurally for use as a garden can be a simple or an elaborate undertaking, but you must always have it checked out first. Bring in an engineer to make sure your beautiful plot does not end up in your living room.

This site had two roofs, which opened up the possibility of gardening on different levels and instantly gave it great interest and great potential. New false floors of steel beams, locked in to the existing walls, provided the structural strength and integrity we needed to make a secure deck. Galvanized steps were welded into position to allow access from one level to another. For added interest, we incorporated water rills which opened out of the edge of the upper deck and shot water out and down to the level below to incorporate the excitement and sound of moving water.

At the higher level, we built a deck on which we installed a circular enclosure of metal and wood screens on tracks; the eight panels could whiz around to open up or block out views around the central dining area. They also provided some shelter against the elements. On this upper deck we put a variety of plants in metal troughs – these doubled up as boundary fences and railings. Often in a roof garden the planting may need to be kept to a minimum because of the problems caused by weight. If the roof has been properly adapted to take increased weight, so much the better. As the soil used in the pots can often add a lot of weight, it is always a good idea to add polystyrene balls to the soil to add air pockets and decrease its mass and hence its weight. Equally, when determining the containers you want to use, do think about the material from which they are made and how much weight they will add to the surface – for example, light steel containers are a better option than solid lead.

Downstairs, on the lower level, a deck was created in an elliptical shape with a shallow trough of water running through it, which echoed the rill on the deck above. Incorporating water in a rooftop scheme can also bring with it weight issues – we forget how heavy water can be in large amounts and how much damage it can cause to structures. For this reason the rills were very shallow and only a small amount of water was pumped through them. The moving water brought reflective qualities to the scheme and broke up the hard landscaping and the decking. Planting on this level was restricted to the sides to limit the weight and also to create an open space that allowed for sun worshipping or ball games. ∎

Opposite: Upstairs is a soothing family area complete with circular swivel-screened room for relaxing, dining or even outdoor showering. Downstairs is given over to play.

Left: Two steel rills jut out from the top walls to create dramatic waterfalls which generate noise and distract the ear from the sound of road traffic. A shimmer of light travels through the lower deck by means of a simple tray of water.

Torpedo

A reluctant, inaccessible space is transformed into a stylish garden for all the family through the use of strong lines, soft planting and structure.

Immense fun can be had In small gardens, when you decide to take complete control of your plot and introduce brand new lines inspired by strong design with graphic shapes. It can be as joyful as going to the beach with buckets and spades and creating cities of sand castles linked together by walls. It's the ultimate controlling of form.

In most city and suburban plots, it is you who creates the rules regarding the style and content of your garden – the only limiting factors are the shape of your boundaries and the lie of your land. Best of all is when your site is already inherently interesting – such as this one which included a dramatic drop from the house and patio level to the rest of the garden – as some of your work is already done for you.

At first glance, such drops can appear to make the garden itself seem an inhospitable, and possibly dangerous, place – and the remedy is apparently difficult. In this case, although the garden was not physically removed by a great distance from the house, it appeared to be so inaccessible that it didn't inspire a great desire in the visitor to get out into it and explore. The trick here was to turn what seemed to be a disadvantage into the opportunity to create a really unique garden – one that would not exist at all had it not been for this apparently unfriendly starting point.

Terracing, using interesting shapes and different materials, was the key here in creating a successful and inviting landscape. Terracing is an excellent way of carving usable, level spaces on sloping sites and has been a feature of farming in mountainous regions for thousands of years. Some of the most successful gardens have been created on a series of terraces running down hillsides – each area can be developed with its own distinctive character and for a variety of uses.

The graphic lines of this garden were based on torpedo shapes – long, straight stretches of strong lines that resolved themselves in equally strong curved ends. The shape was repeated over and over – in the lines of the structure of a new room for the garden (See Dens, p.68), in the shape of the terraced raised beds and, finally, even in the detail of the lawn edging.

In contrast, a circular staircase was the central structure of the garden. It was the main link between the various levels and looked inviting and fun to use.

To add interest to the scheme, all the surfaces of the three main levels created by our new shapes were all treated differently. New paving was introduced into the enclosed space at the top level. On the second level, a raised bed was constructed to house low planting, while the third level enclosed a lawn, which acted as a carpet and a foil to everything else that went on in the garden. When you're creating terraces in such strongly graphic shapes, it's a good idea to outline them to reinforce their strength and show exactly what you're doing. The owner of this site was pregnant when the design was evolving and this led to the development of the colour scheme for the mosaic tile borders and retaining walls – baby pink and baby blue.

Although the shape of the garden had been initially difficult, exerting firm control on its form by introducing deliberate, defined levels with strong, new graphic lines created a cohesive whole. ∎

Opposite: The torpedo or capsule shape of the main structure is echoed in the shape of the terraced raised beds and bottom lawn area. Your eye follows the main line and is constantly led downwards creating a view of the garden.

Below left: A low bed on the main terrace is again built in a capsule shape and planted with fun lollipop-type specimens.

Below right: Planting disappears underneath the garden structure creating a truly multi-level plot.

Poles apart

A garden in south London had a background vista of high-rise flats. The forms and shapes of these dwelling places were echoed in a stepped garden on a sloping site.

The surrounding landscape can have a huge effect on the design for your garden and it is very important to acknowledge this and to spend time observing the area before you even begin planning. On a site like this one, in a gently sloping valley, which both overlooks and is overlooked by its surroundings, it is especially important to consider the effects your plans will have on the wider landscape and vice versa. If the landscape beyond your plot is in view, you should carefully consider the elements of your design so that you are not creating a blot on the landscape, but equally, you could also aim to steal the landscape and incorporate it into your design rather than blocking it out. The obligation here was to regard the garden as not only the possession of its owners but also as an integral part of the overall landscape.

With sloping gardens, peripheral boundaries that act on a practical level to keep people or animals in or out can become visually redundant when viewed from a distance. If your topography is dramatic, their existence becomes a visual by-line. The features that fall within your immediate and middle distance sight lines become all the more telling.

So when it comes to creating an interesting garden on a somewhat enclosed valley site such as this, the defining lines need to fall within it – either running along the slopes in gentle curves or in more organized, stepped patterns. If you walk through the garden and observe the potential routes and vistas out from and back towards the house and then ponder on these observations for a while, you have a far better chance of developing a sympathetic scheme – one that floats in the space rather than screams from it.

The views from the valley that held this garden were full of vertical lines; severe in the case of the tower blocks on one side and gentle in the beautiful mature trees on the other. The desire of the client was to create harmony with these surroundings, and to bring a sense of drama into the garden. We also needed to create private areas, which seemed to demand a sculptural quality that would further reinforce the link between the garden and its surroundings. We used old, reclaimed telegraph poles as the dominant vertical features in the garden, which looked natural in their setting even when they were set into the ground at different levels to achieve a stepped effect down from the house. Around these poles, we

created a series of open buildings (see Dens, p.70), which were raised above the ground to create level sites for practical use; their openness and varying elevated heights enhanced the feeling that they were floating in the landscape.

Much attention was given to the roofs of these structures. They were deliberately finished in wood, which gave the secondary appearance of elevated platforms on different levels when they were viewed from other dwellings above them. A spirit of openness prevailed and, as you moved through the garden, new views were formed, framed by a series of verticals. Glass was occasionally incorporated in the frames to retain the views and open feeling while also providing some physical shelter.

The original slope of the land was retained and cultivated to create areas of trees, shrubs and even gently sloping lawns, but the incline had been refined into a more manageable scheme with the open platforms providing level, and therefore functional, areas. The planting scheme worked well to provide a unifying factor, echoing the mature trees in the distance, and bringing another element of cohesiveness into the design. ∎

Opposite: Telegraph poles of various heights were set in the ground almost like an army trudging up a mountainside. Although supporting a series of platforms and roofs their tops were not sheared off uniformly, adding to a sense of drama and reminding us that they once stood proudly as trees.

Right: A set of simple wooden steps leads from one terrace to another.

Far right: The poles travel upwards through the structure and out over the top.

High gloss

A divided courtyard garden is transformed into a cohesive entertaining area by linking separate and untidy spaces through a set of steps and uniformity of materials.

Creating levels in a garden is not all about improving accessibility. Sometimes, different levels are expressed in walling and raised beds and in a scale which is relative to the space. This is often an advantage in terms of ease of construction, and one of the main areas of interest can come from the materials chosen to create them – in their actual building and cladding and in terms of the plants cultivated there.

Courtyard gardens can be great fun as long as you don't expect too much from them and try to put in everything but the kitchen sink. But they are the ideal place for raised beds. These are, in effect, large window boxes – troughs filled with as much growing medium as possible and planted up. In a confined situation, they are generally used at the edge of the site – where they won't clutter the space – and they act not only as places for choice plants, but they can also double up as seating, which is useful in restricted spots.

This garden was one that was full of problems. Tall brick walls on different levels stepped up in front of a narrow, sloping plot. The garden was divided into two areas, with walls running away from each other at uncomfortable angles. When you're surrounded by a small, awkwardly-shaped site with austere, high walling that seems to press in on you from every angle, you really have to take a step back to see how to relieve the feeling of oppression and turn the elements of height and enclosure to advantage.

A cohesive design had to be developed to link everything together, including a multitude of materials, and decorating most certainly had to take place. The garden was intended to be a party garden, the ultimate outdoor entertaining experience; this cold, narrow passageway of uninspiring space somehow needed to be transformed into a chic and exciting garden.

Our first job was to make the second of the two areas accessible and inviting by introducing new steps down to it. These were to be a central focal point, rather than to be hidden around the corner, and would indicate to people that they could actually move freely throughout the plot. Secondly, a new low wall was created which would snake around the site. This wall was covered in black mosaic tiles and created a new link between the different levels as it developed into a radical curve which acted as a backdrop to the steps and pursued its own gentle way that didn't follow the austere, angular lines of the existing rear wall. At its uppermost level, it formed a new enclosure for plants (see Planting, p.102).

The tall brick walls around the patio area were clad in wood and stepped to varying heights to add interest. Circular openings were cut out of the cladding and five mirrors were inserted in the gaps to create further excitement. A large circular hole in another wall had a graphic quality during the day, but at night it acted as a screen for projected images, which emerged from the house. This circular form was echoed elsewhere in the garden and became a unifying theme that integrated all the levels and the different materials together. Blue glass lenses – illuminated from beneath by fibre-optic lighting, which would flash gently on and off – were sunk into the ground decking. These lights were then repeated at different heights, set into the mosaic-tiled walls adding another, more subtle echo of the levels in the garden. Finally, all the changes in levels were softened by abundant planting. ∎

Opposite: A curved wall clad in square black mosaic winds its way through the garden and links the two levels together. The wall is planted at the top and the bottom to minimize the hard effect.

Left above: A sleek set of chairs and table indicates the use of this chic outdoor space

Left below: Pots of rosemary on the new steps soften the architectural features.

Case study
Box of tricks

At first sight, this garden appeared to be one of the most challenging we had encountered on *Home Front in the Garden* in a long while. This was mostly due to the fact that it was a very unusual site, and for two different reasons: firstly, it was adjacent to the family house, not running directly away from it or behind it, as is most often the case; secondly, the plot was on a vast scale and was overlooked by twenty-three other properties. Local rumours suggested that the site had been a tennis court for previous generations, but what we were sure of was that a previous owner had used the site to grow fruit and vegetables, which meant that there was probably some good, well-cultivated soil to work with. At first glance, however, we were not so positive. Long neglected, whatever it had been previously, it had now reverted to a field full of briars, couch grass, bindweed and nettles – all over 2m (6ft) tall.

Case study
Box of tricks

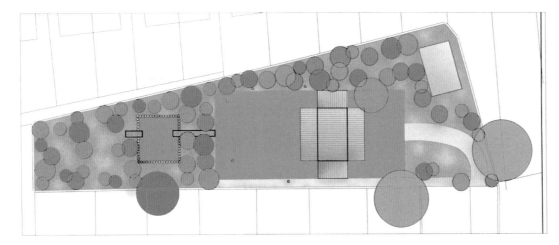

I always encourage people to live with their existing garden before they decide on a new design for it, not just so they can get a feel for what they have and learn where the sunlight falls in the plot, etc., but also so that they can see what plants, if any, come up over the different seasons. By doing this you can learn where to site your patio for optimum sun, but also you are not in danger of digging over the ground and losing some potentially beautiful plant you didn't know was there. In this garden, however, the only useful existing vegetation that we could retain in the new scheme was a lonely apple tree. But, although the garden was bordered only by low walls, we had the real advantage that there were some beautiful ash and willow trees in neighbouring gardens that almost seemed to belong to our site and created an already established green backdrop to the new design.

Using the space

The owners of this garden were a young family who were used to a much smaller space, having previously lived in one of the houses that overlooked their new home. Matthew and Kim were creative people, working as trend spotters and consultants to multi-national organizations; they were very design literate, and they also had a real appreciation for nature. For them, the garden needed to be an invigorating space in which they could grow plants and socialize; it also needed to be a safe place that the two children, Emily and Chloe, could enjoy.

Despite a generous budget, their investment would have to stretch a long way – there was much to be done in this large space. One of their requirements included creating some sort of pavilion – an outdoor building that could be opened up when the garden was in use to create a stimulating retreat. They also wanted the children to have their own play area and were keen for the family's love of trees and bright colours to be reflected in the planting scheme.

Design and materials

The design for this garden evolved over a number of months and was inspired by the history of the site and the enthusiasm of the family. It was characterized by economy – economy of materials, structure and form. A huge lawn across the garden allowed plenty of space for the children to have fun and play games without coming to any harm.

At one end of the lawn, we placed what appeared to be a large wooden box, but, in fact, this structure had many different uses and forms. Its design was based on that of a shipping container – broad, rectangular, uncompromising, and strong when closed. The idea was that all of the sides would be able to fall away to the ground to reveal a bright, airy room inside, which had a second skin of wire-mesh screens. If the owners wanted privacy or screening from the elements, any combination of the walls could be erected in a matter of seconds. A spring mechanism, similar to that used in horseboxes, was incorporated so that the metal-framed and wooden-clad walls would lower gently on the exertion of slight pressure. Once they reached the ground, the walls then served another purpose – as hardwearing decks that surrounded the building.

The room inside was laid out with a cream, rubber-crumb floor that added soft and luxurious contrast to the other, slightly harder materials.

The room was also fitted with electricity so that it could become a real den and place of retreat – opening up the possibilities of making it a place to watch television, listen to music, or even to plug in a computer with games for the children.

At the far end of the garden, we erected a square fort simply by placing legions of telegraph poles upright in the ground. The entrance to the fort was a tunnel that was constructed from galvanized steel grills, giving a simple, space-age quality to an otherwise traditional construction. The theme of natural wood was echoed throughout the garden; more telegraph poles were used as both seating and as aesthetic, vertical constructions, some ringed by neon light to create a vibrant night-time setting.

Planting

I decided that the planting scheme for this garden should be dominated by trees, inspired by the fact that, once the site had been cleared, we could appreciate the many beautiful trees that were planted in the neighbouring gardens, some of which had weeping branches overhanging our plot. Free of brambles, bindweed and couch grass, our site became a haven rather than a jungle. Once the lawn had been laid as the central 'carpeted' area that formed a setting for our structures, choosing the trees was our next job. We decided against

using large species in this garden, because we felt that the large trees that already existed in the neighbouring gardens were sufficient to create a wonderful backdrop of mature planting. Instead, we decided to use smaller species, such as rowans and birches, especially in the area behind the children's fort where they would create a sense of mystery and intrigue. At other strategic points throughout the space, trees were used in borders and even in the lawn, to create a feeling of privacy as well as to offset the dominance of the surrounding domestic architecture by drawing the eye back into the garden.

All of the family had a love of bright colours, but rather than lose the effect of the natural materials used for the various constructions, we decided that the planting scheme was the perfect place to reflect this and bring colour to the garden, rather than paint. The straight borders that hugged the perimeter walls and pathways were planted with flowering shrubs, such as lavatera, potentilla, hydrangea, caryopteris, ceanothus and lavender. A number of large, purple-leaved hazels were also used for their deep rich colours, along with the occasional grouping of herbaceous plants, such as achilleas and hemerocallis.

Above: The garden revealed – a large wooden box whose walls gently fall down to become usable decks. A second skin is created by the use of wood and stainless steel mesh screens which give a sense of privacy without blocking out all the light.

Above right: A swing was made from wood and steel and adds a fun element for the children. Natural materials abounded in this garden – the beautiful soft cedar clad metal frames to create moving walls.

Case study
Box of tricks

Above left: When the garden isn't in use the room can be simply folded away. Lawn runs right up to the edge of the box so maintenance is relatively easy.

Above right: A telegraph pole supports a piece of scaffolding tube from which a chained swing is hung.

Opposite: Views are continually framed in the modern, sleek 50s-inspired garden room. A cream-coloured rubber crumb floor completes the textural feel. Simple furnishings added a stylish touch.

One of the long narrow beds was backed by an ugly concrete garden wall that ranged in aspect from full sun to light shade. This gave us a great opportunity to plant a wide selection of lovely evergreen and deciduous climbers that would provide wonderful bursts of colour through flower and foliage all year round. The plants we selected ranged from honeysuckles (*Lonicera*) and ivies (*Hedera*) in the lightly shaded areas, to the flowering abundance of *Solanum crispum* 'Glasnevin', *Campsis* and passionflower (*Passiflora*), and fruiting grapes (*Vitis*) and figs (*Ficus*), in the sunnier zones. ∎

Case study
Box of tricks

Above left: Steel discs coated in enamel are placed on the lawn to provide temporary colour to amuse the children.

Above right: Metal grill, often used as a flooring, creates an entrance tunnel

Opposite: A majestic weeping willow, a simple steel and wooden building form a soft architectural background for fun and games.

Selected plant list

Achillea Hoffnung (syn. A. 'Great Expectations')
Herbaceous perennial. Sun, moist but well-drained soil. H 75cm (30in), S 60cm (24in).

Aucuba japonica 'Crotonifolia'
(Spotted laurel) Evergreen shrub. Sun/shade but prefers partial shade, any soil except waterlogged. H and S 3m (10ft).

Aucuba japonica 'Rozannie'
Evergreen shrub. Sun/partial shade/shade, any soil except waterlogged. H and S 1m (3ft).

Campsis x tagliabuana 'Madame Galen'
(Trumpet creeper) Deciduous climber. Sun, moderately fertile, moist but well-drained soil. H 10m (30ft) or more.

Caryopteris x clandonensis 'Heavenly Blue'
Deciduous shrub. Sun, moderately fertile, light, well-drained soil. H 1m (3ft), S 1.5m (5ft).

Ceanothus x delileanus 'Topaze'
(Californian lilac) Deciduous shrub. Sun, fertile, well-drained soil, sheltered from strong, cold winds. H and S 1.5m (5ft).

Choisya ternata
(Mexican orange blossom) Evergreen shrub. Sun, fertile, well-drained soil. H and S 2.5m (8ft).

Corylus maxima 'Purpurea'
(Purple hazel) Deciduous shrub. Sun, fertile, well-drained soil, ideal for chalky soils. H 6m (20ft), S 5m (15ft).

Hebe vernicosa
Evergreen shrub. Sun, well-drained soil. H 60cm (2ft), S 1.2m (4ft).

Hedera canariensis 'Gloire de Marengo'
Evergreen climber. Shade tolerant but prefers light, sheltered wall, moist but well-drained soil. H 4m (12ft).

Hedera helix 'Little Diamond'
(Ivy) Evergreen climber. Tolerates a range of conditions but prefers sun, shelter from cold wind, and fertile, moist but well-drained soil. H and S 30cm (12in).

Hosta fortunei 'Aureomarginata'
Herbaceous perennial. Full/partial shade, fertile, moist but well-drained soil with shelter from cold, drying winds. H 55cm (22in), S 1m (3ft).

Hydrangea involucrata 'Hortensis'
Deciduous shrub. Sun/partial shade with shelter from cold, drying winds, moist but well-drained, moderately fertile, humus-rich soil. H 1m (3ft), S 2m (6ft).

Hydrangea macrophylla 'Maculata'
Deciduous shrub. Sun/partial shade with shelter from cold, drying winds, moist but well-drained, moderately fertile, humus-rich soil. H 1m (3ft), S 1.5m (5ft).

Hypericum 'Hidcote'
Evergreen/semi-evergreen shrub. Sun/partial shade, moist but well-drained soil. H 1.2m (4ft), S 1.5m (5ft).

Lavandula angustifolia
Evergreen shrub. Sun, moderately fertile, well-drained soil. H 1m (3ft), S 1.2m (4ft).

Lavatera x clementii 'Rosea' (syn. L. olbia 'Rosea')
(Mallow) Semi-evergreen shrub. Sun, light, moderately fertile, well-drained soil. H and S 2m (6ft).

Lonicera x heckrottii 'Goldflame'
(Honeysuckle) Deciduous climber. Partial shade, fertile, humus-rich, moist but well-drained soil. H 5m (15ft).

Passiflora 'Amethyst' (syn. P. 'Lavender Lady')
(Passionflower) Semi-evergreen climber. Sun with shelter from cold, drying winds, moderately fertile, moist but well-drained soil. Tender (may survive temperatures down to 0°C if the wood has been well-ripened in summer). H 4m (12ft) or more.

Physocarpus opulifolius 'Dart's Gold'
Deciduous shrub. Sun, fertile, moist but well-drained, preferably acid, soil. H 2m (6ft), S 2.5m (8ft).

Potentilla fruticosa 'Goldfinger'
Deciduous shrub. Sun, poor to moderately fertile, well-drained soil. H 1m (3ft), S 1.5m (5ft).

Potentilla fruticosa 'Jackman's Variety'
Deciduous shrub. Sun, poor to moderately fertile, well-drained soil. H 1m (3ft), S 1.5m (5ft).

Rosa rugosa 'Alba'
(White hedgehog rose) Deciduous shrub. Sun, fertile, well-drained soil. H and S 1–2.5m (3–8ft).

Salvia officinalis
(Common sage) Evergreen shrub. Full sun/light dappled shade, light, moderately fertile, moist but well-drained soil. H 80cm (32in), S 1m (3ft).

Solanum crispum 'Glasnevin'
(Chilean potato tree) Evergreen/semi-evergreen climber. Sun, moderately fertile, moist but well-drained, neutral to slightly alkaline soil. H 6m (20ft).

Viburnum davidii
Evergreen shrub. Sun/semi-shade, deep, fertile, not too dry soil. H and S 1–1.5m (3–5ft).

Vinca minor 'Atropurpurea'
(Lesser periwinkle) Evergreen shrub. Sun/partial shade, any soil but not too dry. H 10–20cm (4–8in), S indefinite.

Enclosures

Enclosures

In the past, enclosures were constructed to break up large gardens into smaller, more manageable areas. The first illustrations of this that come to mind are the traditional walled gardens for fruit and vegetables and the separate gardens that were often made as themed areas, or to house groups of plants, as in rose and herb gardens. They added to the sense of a journey through a landscape and created a little bit of mystery and intrigue. When suburban gardens were first developed, while maintenance areas and fruit and vegetable plots may have been hidden behind a hedge, openness was the key – showing off the amount of space that was available.

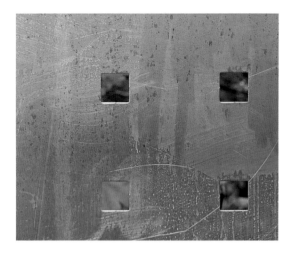

But by most people's definition, the garden is itself an enclosure; a place that's divided off from the rest of the world to create a refuge – an environment that, ideally, creates a secluded feel. It is possible, though, to create more special and individualistic havens within larger spaces. As our way of living and our relationship with the world around us has changed so radically, so too has our definition of seclusion and our appreciation of outdoor space. We have become very aware of our immediate environment inside the house and outside and have strongly defined ideas on how to use them. Our ideals for both are often characterized by carving up an open space to create areas where we can relax, privately or in groups, so as to indulge in time spent winding down alone or in social gatherings.

Material considerations

Recently, we have become aware of the inherent beauty of different materials and especially in the relationship between materials and planting. It has long been acceptable to admire the beauty of a red brick wall, a flint wall or a dry-stone wall that housed plants and to appreciate their symbiotic relationship. The value of a brick wall in retaining heat and helping to ripen fruit grown against it has long been understood, and the fact that the plants, in turn, draw attention to the beauty of the material has probably always been appreciated. We now realize, with the increasing value placed on our living spaces, that every material that we use in a garden,

be it hard or soft, has a part to play. Part of that role and, indeed, one of the main obligations of the material, is to be beautiful as well as functional – to withstand the elements, to enclose whatever we want to be enclosed, and to support whatever we wish to support in terms of planting. And so today's designers consider their materials very, very carefully and they have never been better served. The multitude of materials that provide opportunities to create enclosures has never been greater. Stone, brick, concrete, metal, wood, glass, Perspex, wire, acrylic and rubber are all in evidence; used singly or in combination; they can all work to great effect either as stand-alone objects of beauty, or in conjunction with planting schemes. Each has individual qualities that can make them suitable or, of course, unsuitable for a particular scheme. And when used with technology, they can help create entertainment and magic.

The decisions regarding which materials are to be used for constructing an enclosure should be carefully made, and made only after we have explored in full the qualities of the material in question. Only when we do this can we create schemes that are both unique and uniquely rewarding.

Creating a haven

When emphasis is placed on the needs of the individual, individual spaces that are defined by enclosures can create unique havens. And a haven is what an enclosure is all about. It is a place that we create as a sanctuary –

a place of refuge and retreat. It may be formed by hard landscaping, but can also be created with plants, as in a living screen of trees and shrubs or hedging. This can be very rewarding – a circular yew hedge, for example, with an occasional seat set into an alcove can be a real retreat. But if you don't have years to wait for a hedge to grow, you can create your own surrounds instantly by building circular brick or wooden enclosed rooms, which can also incorporate seating. Then you can sit back and enjoy the space while the plants grow up around you to clothe it.

But a haven need not be totally isolated – it can be constructed incorporating openings in a patterned way, or by deliberately allowing light to pour through. Constructed in this way, the main function of the material is to provide shelter and if a clear material is used – such as glass, acrylic or Perspex – it will also allow you a view of the rest of your garden from your retreat. The important thing is to get the balance right, to define from the outset what you are trying to achieve with the relationships between materials and planting. A stark wooden room can work very well in a garden, if that's what you desire, but maybe something heavily planted with only occasional, emerging hints of the background material is your preference.

Be sensible with the proportion and the shapes of your enclosures. Be sure that they fit into the overall scheme and that they are not inherently awkward. Simple shapes, such as circles, squares and gentle ellipses, work well.

Try to include seating or ground-covering surfaces that encourage lying down and looking up. Create an ambience inside that encourages relaxation or meditation. If simplicity is the aim, maybe include just a single specimen – offset rather than planted centrally – on which you can meditate. If your enclosure is in a built-up area, try to make the walls as tall as you possibly can (within local authority guidelines) so that when you look up, the sky is your vista and your mind can be freed of any outside influence. One specimen tree or even a stark piece of architecture can lead the eye upwards. While rest may be paramount, the idea of socializing – inviting friends into your secret place – can also be appealing. ■

Jenga

Jenga is a game in which two or more people construct a tower from simple wooden blocks, in this garden architecture and fun was achieved with this wooden and perspex enclosure.

Enclosures need not be rigid, permanent structures; they can easily be semi-permeable and can be made from all sorts of different materials. Don't think of an enclosure as a one-hundred-percent barrier – it can be a visual trick, an almost complete piece of walling, hedging or fencing that gives a sense of shelter rather than a feeling of being totally enclosed.

In this garden, the clients expressed a desire for an outdoor room but with the specific theme of a shower, so I needed to design an enclosure that could provide this, as well as privacy and a feeling of intimacy. I wanted to play with the idea of circles and squares surrounding each other and to create the enclosures out of natural materials.

The first line of structure was formed by great slabs of stone set into the ground around an inner sanctum. It was modelled on Stonehenge and needed plenty of space around it to allow the appreciation of the innate beauty and power of this natural material. The stones served a dual purpose here; they were also used as a framing device. As you walked around the garden, or even as you observed the stones while moving through the rooms indoors, the views of them – and the appreciation of their structure in relation to the garden beyond – changed constantly.

Part of the fun of being a designer is looking at the ingredients available to you in different ways. Having recently sourced top-quality, brand-new railway sleepers for use as a dining room table, I hit on their potential for use as walling within a garden and on the idea of building with them to create separate enclosures in a wider space. The real enclosure in this garden, therefore, was created with railway sleepers, which were placed on firm concrete foundations with metal rods running through to provide additional strength and make them safe. On the inside of this enclosure, movable Perspex panels were placed in different, colourful configurations. As the sun shone through them or, alternatively, when they were illuminated from the inside at night, they created a stained-glass-like effect, casting vibrant colour shades from the inside out. The overall effect of this enclosure was to create an outdoor room within the garden that was fun, distinctive but one that didn't dominate the entire space. ■

Opposite: Observing materials as they are and appreciating their shape, form and inherent beauty was key to this square enclosure – adding perspex sheets to the wooden blocks added a sense of colourful daring. Surrounding this structure again by upright slabs of sentry-like stones created a real sense of timeless intrigue.

Above: Blue skies are often the key to enjoyment of a garden – especially if they encourage you to lie down and look up and appreciate plant and form against an open expanse.

Left: The coloured perspex could be slotted in or out and used in any combination as required; to open up the enclosure or to create a sense of mystery.

Trad Mod

An old garden with a new twist is revealed when a new enclosure is created by the addition of a simple curved wall clad in reflective stainless steel opening out to a separate section.

By building additional structures in gardens, you can also create the effect of the new structure working with existing features and forming enclosures. At the end of this large garden was an area that contained a swimming pool. A rather ugly swimming pool enclosure had recently been added in the form of a cover that slid back and forth to create seasonal protection. Its municipal appearance was not a pretty sight, especially in its new context of a genteel Repton-inspired landscape. So we needed to find a way of enclosing the pool in a more aesthetically pleasing way – and one that would also provide a private, self-enclosed area around the pool that was separate from the rest of the garden.

I decided to construct a curved wall clad in sheets of mirror-polished stainless steel that would be a feature in its own right as well as serving a practical purpose. An oval, walk-through, central opening was cut into the wall to create a reflective and mysterious focal point and an entrance into a now hidden part of the garden. The wall worked in conjunction with an existing hedge to act as a screen and to create a boundary within the garden, but was made to stand out from the hedge and curve towards the viewer. Its gentle, c-shaped form invited attention, and its shiny, mirrored surface created a sleek resolution. The garden and the viewer are reflected back onto themselves, albeit in a relatively surreal way, as the metal plays with images and light much as a Hall of Mirrors does with the human form at a funfair. The pool was now neatly tucked away in its own enclosed space leaving the new garden to be enjoyed without blemish. ■

Opposite: Like a hall of mirors in a funfair your eye can play a trick on you; firstly by observing the surreal images created by reflections of garden greenery on a different plane, and then by the reality of more garden space beyond the new entrance hole.

Left and below: The architecture of a pool enclosure is disguised by framing it in an interesting shape. You are enticed down to examine a separate area as if through a looking glass. Surreal imagery is created through reflective metal.

Curvy

The construction of walling within a garden deflects the eye from straight boundaries of wooden fences and old hedges, carving out new space from old.

Occasionally, an enclosure in a garden is all about getting away from or disguising the boundaries of the property. The majority of gardens are of a uniform shape – generally square or rectangular – and are mainly viewed from within the property, be it a house or an office. A requirement of good design is to make the shape of that space work for you, rather than to allow it to dominate; the determining factors in making it work here would be the use of line and form.

The shape of this garden, and therefore the structures within it, were influenced by the curves of the female form. The idea was to create separate rooms in curved shapes that met in the centre of the garden at the point where there was an existing tree. The clients had initially requested that the tree be removed, but I felt that was important that it should remain as the linchpin that linked the individual rooms together and made sense of them. In effect, the enclosures drew attention to the tree, which, although it appeared initially to be dominant and awkwardly placed, was actually the heart of the garden. It provided a restful focus and reinforced the tranquillity and overarching privacy that was required of the enclosures.

In keeping with the central importance of the living tree, which almost demanded the use of natural materials, this enclosure was to be made out of wood and

we decided on a beautiful western red cedar, which is an exceptionally weather-resistant softwood. A double layer of red cedar was mounted on a swirling metal frame, which created a sculptural composition that was perfectly in keeping with the sensual theme of the garden. It was an exciting structure, but a very difficult construction to achieve; rather than rising at right angles to the ground, it leaned on both sides to give a great sense of energy to the curves of the overall form.

The internal structures, based on a framework of metal, meant that each piece of timber had to be cut to size by a small army of joiners on site. The timber also had to be held above the ground to avoid deterioration of the wood, since, however inherently durable a timber is, it inevitably rots on prolonged contact with the soil moisture. The use of western red cedar in this garden meant that treatment with preservatives or oils was not necessary – the wood contains its own oils which protect against pest damage.

The top capping, which would ensure that rainwater would be shed from the cut ends of the timbers, was again set at a different angle to accentuate the flowing lines. The void between the two layers of timber allowed room for the cantilevered construction of the concrete and wooden benches that provided private and secluded seating areas within the enclosures. ■

Opposite: A curved pathway leads you to a new opening – a new room within your garden room. The walls are constructed from western red cedar set at three different angles to create not only background and backdrop, but also sculptural interest.

Above left: A sense of movement is achieved by simply looking up and following the line of the new enclosure.

Above right: Architectural lighting is set into the gently sloped wooden wall. The lights act as architectural features as well as practical solutions for nighttime enjoyment.

Igloo

Exploring the potential of using a familiar material in a different way led to the creation of a new shape in outdoor enclosures – walk-through buildings that were constructed by spraying concrete around steel frames.

Opposite: Concrete paving slabs, rooms and containers for water are linked together by gravel and planting to create a surreal set that owes its inspiration more to sci-fi movies than traditional gardens.

Above: Enclosures can be gentle areas like these slightly sunken patios surrounded by wide and narrow steps. They provide places to encourage people to gather together to sit and eat or stand and dance.

When covered structures are used throughout the garden, and not only at the far end or against walls, it can be most satisfying to design them so that they do another job – that of creating a sheltered space that can be used as a gathering area without blocking the passage of people or obscuring the longer view for the eye.

Here, the concrete, walk-through buildings were used to allow access through the garden – and invite exploration. As open structures, they allow you to enter, sit down on the soft rubber flooring and then admire the view onwards to the back of the garden and also appreciate the reverse view back along the pathway to the house from which you came.

Concrete is a material that has been used by generations of architects in creative ways, but gardeners have been reluctant to appreciate its potential to the full. It can be used to create furniture, seating areas, water features and buildings in organic, sculptural, and flowing lines. Although a hard, rigid material, concrete is, in fact, a material that can be easily manipulated, coloured, or used in bold, varied shapes. One method of using concrete to create constructions with more fluid lines is to spray it on to metal frames. It was this technique that we used to create the flowing shapes in this garden.

A whole seating area was used in the design to suggest its own sense of enclosure, but this was achieved by sinking the space into the ground rather than by surrounding it by high walls. Different tiers were sunk below the level of the rest of the garden to create a cosy, enveloping feeling, by bringing the user down to the level of a planting that is different and unusual; this gives the impression not only of being enclosed by the structure, but also by the plants. In this case, the jungle feel was exploited to the maximum, so that it added to the 'crawl-through' feeling of a tropical rainforest. But the area could also be used for entertainment, as it was also perfect as a self-contained dance floor.

One vital thing to remember, though, if you are planning to sink any open structure, be it a walk-through building, or a seating area like the one here, is that you may need to fit a drain combined with a sump pump to ensure that your feature does not become a self-contained pool! ∎

Cinescape

Apart from gardening, one of the nation's favourite pastimes is going to the cinema, so the idea was to combine both pleasures in this communal garden shared by the residents of five flats.

Opposite: A sunken pit surrounded by raised beds of different levels, a glass corridor and a pink projection house creates a cosmopolitan viewing area.

Right: The glass corridor creates an access point from the car park to the cinema but it is also an effective boundary wall without diluting natural sunlight.

Below: The projection room is a circular tower with a letterbox opening – all painted a frivolous candy pink.

Enclosures are usually created for a specific purpose – either for privacy, to screen out other people, or just to create a different environment and atmosphere in one part of the garden without affecting the style of the rest of it. This garden was used communally by a group of young residents who shared the space that was attached to their complex of apartments.

The residents were a vibrant bunch – all relatively new to gardening – who loved the idea of gathering socially in the outdoor space next to their building. They wanted to continue the pastime that they enjoyed best indoors – watching movies together – but in an outside space. So an enclosed, sunken area seemed the perfect solution. This enclosure was bordered on one side by a glass corri-dor that led to the car park, and which included a circular pink tower housing a DVD player that beamed images across the paved floor onto a white metal movie screen.

The primary influences were the 1920s and '30s Art Deco architecture and the colours of Miami Beach that were used in combination with an appreciation of outdoor living. These styles were adapted to fit in with an appreciation of contemporary life and its entertainment systems in an urban environment. A surround-sound system was installed and the whole hi-tech, contemporary effect was softened by planting on three different levels. At night, the whole area came to life with sparkling images, enhanced by the light sources within the glass brick wall. ∎

Coastal suburban

A very large open space near the seaside is broken up into distinct areas simply by the use of shape, either created as flat surfaces on the ground or in three-dimensional ways as walk-through frames or archways.

Enclosures can be simply constructed as visual tricks and with shapes on the ground as opposed to solid, vertical structures. This long garden near the sea in Essex was divided by means of line and shape. We positioned the living area immediately outside the back door for practical reasons, and the space was indicated by circles of decking wood on slightly different levels that were enclosed by lush, vigorous planting. Two of the levels contained curved wooden seats on metal frames, which lead the eye continually onwards. The final definition for the social space was a large oval structure that both framed a view and acted as a lounging device. This served to complete the patio area but also to link it to the garden beyond.

Although, in this garden, the enclosure isn't a physical barrier, the combination of the flat shape of the circles and the three-dimensional bulk of the vegetative growth acted to create the desired effect. The oval frame increased the feeling of enclosure while also opening up the possibility of more adventure to come.

The next section of the garden was dominated by a large, elliptical lawn running from left to right. At the end of this, a brick and steel archway in a modern form was constructed to create the sense of a further second room in the garden. The children's playing area was located beyond this archway to give them their own space and privacy and to separate it from the rest of the garden, while still keeping the area safely within view.

The first part of the garden was to be used for immediate outdoor living for the whole family and friends, for entertaining and having people gathering in groups on the different decks. The second part was intended be a 'traditional' garden with lots of beautiful planting surrounding a long, elliptical lawn and the third part, defined by the columned entrance, was designed purely as a space for the children. Within this garden and the three separate and defined spaces, the visual and physical combine to create different senses of enclosure without diminishing the potential of what lies beyond. ■

Opposite: Circles, curves and ovals made from deck, low benches, walk-through frames and brick and steel archways create an illusion of movement throughout the garden.

Above left: The eye-shaped opening doubles as a sun lounger as it gently rocks on a central pivot to allow unconventional enjoyment of a piece of garden structure.

Above top: A firepit made from brick surrounded by a low curving wall doubles as seating.

Above bottom: The metal frame clad in wood makes up the step-through and the curved seats also act as a boundary to the circular decks.

Case study
Elevation

In a tiny backyard in Birmingham we needed to create a chic, stylish entertaining area which would also be an extension of the client's newly renovated home. When we first arrived, the site, however, didn't have the same aspirations. The small plot had very little in it and had even less style – the existing design was based around brick paving down a side passage and a lawn that had long since gone to seed. The entire site had the additional problem of sloping upwards towards a focal point of a neglected shed – a thriving buddleia was about the only sign of plant life. Just think of a *Coronation Street* garden and that's what we had.

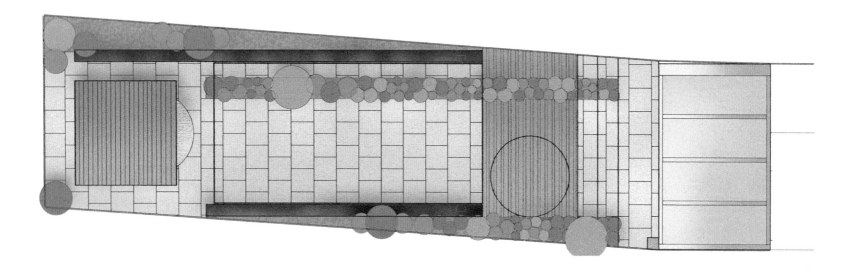

The owner of this Birmingham garden was an
upwardly mobile, Midlands florist who was very
style and design conscious and who greatly valued
his leisure time and wanted to make the most of it.
So, for this reason, he was keen to create an
ultimate outdoor space that could be used to relax
and socialize in. The requirement was to create
something that seemed to drip from the pages of a
glossy magazine, which would include a spa pool,
seating, some sort of cover or shelter and, on a
practical level, a shed. He wanted to include some
planting in the garden, and had expressed a
preference for exotics, which would reflect his
profession and personal taste. He had taken into
consideration that exotics would need heat for
much of the year, particularly in inclement weather,
so had decided he wanted to build a conservatory
in which he could house some of the more
tender species when required. This caused great
excitement as it meant that we had huge scope
for the design and our plant palette could
be much broader than usual.

Design and materials

In a year of many design projects for television this
was the garden that gave me most problems. To try
and transform this difficult, uncompromising space
into a chic entertaining area, which would have
different zones from day to night, was going to be a

challenge but I decided that the secret of success
here would be to try to achieve a balance of
features, planting and space. So how do you achieve
excitement, progression, a suitable planting scheme
and an acceptable choice of materials and colours
and co-ordinate all these elements into a cohesive
unit in a small space? We wanted an urban,
outdoor, sophisticated plot, but at the same time we
needed to steer clear of creating a misguided folly.
It was also important not to create something with
great style and quirkiness but without substance, as
the garden had to work in an aesthetic but practical
way. Another difficult challenge, this garden of
contradictions had to be all-singing and all-dancing,
but discreetly so.

As a result of all these problems, the design for
this garden evolved on site during the build – a
dangerous and unadvisable step to take but one
that, fortunately, worked out. So for this build we
allowed ourselves more time than usual and, as the
client was not living in the house and was
preoccupied with business matters and the
restoration of his home, the garden was left to
evolve gently.

As this garden was a sloping site, the existing
levels had to be excavated. This was no mean task,
100 tonnes of soil and subsoil were removed – a
remarkable amount considering the size of the site.
An outbuilding housing a toilet was demolished and

a conservatory was designed in its place which extended right the way across the garden. New white Portland stone paths and patios were laid, which led down the side of the house and also acted as a floor for the conservatory; linking the inside and the outside spaces through the material. The same stone was used to form steps that led to a sunken wooden spa, which was covered when not in use.

Two new boundary walls were built from concrete block which were then rendered and clad in black, glass mosaic tiles. Into these walls was installed the secret of the garden – a mechanical lifting device generally used to hoist vehicles for

engineering works in a garage. The motor was housed in an outbuilding at the end of the garden and the whole structure worked by means of a hydraulic lift which was built into a metal frame. Once tiled, all that was visible of our lifting device were two slits in each wall, which discreetly housed the metal cables. The outhouse at the end of the garden was a rectangular building which was constructed in blue glazed brick and fronted by a stone frieze – the building also had fibre optic lighting running throughout it.

So, on pressing a button the secret of the garden was revealed. A full stone platform complete with garden furnishings, huge terracotta pots and a

Above: Over 100 tonnes of soil and rubble were removed from this tiny site when the original depth of the garden was lowered by almost 2m (6ft). New walls were then installed along the boundary fences which held a mechanical lift that created the desired rising effect. A metal trough was set into the elevated patio and contained a moving bed of plants.

Case study
Elevation

Below and right: Three stages of elevation. During the day our platform is just a step in the garden, but towards the evening, at the push of a button, it gently rises up – along with the pots, furniture and planting – to finally reveal a sunken area below complete with built-in ceiling lights which can be used for private outdoor entertaining.

Case study
Elevation

Below: The dry stone relief, set in the outhouse at the end of the garden, also housed 200 fibre optic lights which at night added a magic twinkle.

Right: The platform half-way up and surrounded by walls which were awaiting their glass mosaic tiles.

Opposite: The spa pool has been incorporated into a decked area to allow plenty of room for people to sit around and enjoy themselves. It could be covered up when not in use to provide additional flooring.

fully planted containerized bed rose 2 metres (6ft) and revealed a sunken room clad with wooden decking below. In effect, we created a temporary outdoor room to create some privacy and a sense of excitement by introducing motor technology into a garden, with every bit of this technology being hidden. The transformation from conventional garden to sleek social area was complete.

Planting

The planting in the garden was containerized in order to keep maintenance to a minimum and because it was not practical to create beds in the

ground as the planting would need to move with the patio.

A beautiful large, feathered, white-stemmed birch (*Betula utilis* var. *jacquemontii*) was set in a terracotta pot on the patio, as were agaves, oranges and clementines. The vibrant orange of the clementines looked great against the black tiled wall, but this and the other tender plants had to be planted in pots so that they could easily be brought inside to be overwintered in the conservatory. We took advantage of the warm microclimate that we created between the high walls and created an oasis garden using plants that might not have flourished elsewhere.

A long trough, which was fixed on the patio and so moved with it, was heavily planted with lush foliage plants such as cannas with shocking pink flowers and zantedeschia, along with a standard fig, purple spiraea, bronze sedge, liriope and bamboo. In the conservatory, the magnificent, tall papyrus reached the roof alongside a very rich, red leaved Ethiopian banana. The buildings were softened by planting – outside the conservatory, a lollipop-shaped Catalpa stood over a bed planted with miscanthus and lavender, and the blue outhouse was surrounded by common birch (*Betula pendula*) and underplanted with ferns. And then it all goes sky high. ■

Case study
Elevation

Right: A sleek, contemporary conservatory replaces an old toilet at the back of the house.

Far right: Furniture was chosen to be both practical and structural. This concrete chair can be left out in all weather, all year round.

Selected plant list

Agave americana
(Century plant)
Tender, evergreen perennial. Slightly acid, moderately fertile, sharply drained soil, full sun. Bring indoors during winter.
H to 2m (6ft), S to 3m (10ft).

Betula utilis var. *jacquemontii*
(Himalayan birch)
Deciduous tree. Full sun or light dappled shade, moderately fertile, moist but well-drained soil. H 18m (60ft), S 10m (30ft).

Canna x *ehemanii*
(syn. *C. iridiflora*
(Indian shot plant)
Tender perennial. Full sun, sheltered site, fertile soil, lift rhizomes for the winter.
H 3m (10ft), S 50cm (20in).

Carex buchananii
(Leatherleaf sedge)
Evergreen perennial sedge. Most soils in sun or partial shade, avoid extremes of wet or dry.
H 50–75cm (20–30in), S 90cm (36in).

Caryopteris x *clandonensis*
'Worcester Gold'
Deciduous shrub. Sun, well-drained soil.
H and S 0.5m (1.5ft).

Catalpa bungei
(Indian bean tree)
Deciduous tree.
Full sun, fertile, moist but well-drained soil.
H and S 10m (30ft).

Citrus reticulata
(Clementine)
Evergreen shrub/tree. Grow in pots in loam-based compost (John Innes No. 2) in full light, shaded from hot sun. Bring indoors during winter.
H 2–8m (6–25ft), S1.m–3m (5–10ft).

Cupressus sempervirens
(Italian cypress)
Evergreen conifer. Full sun, any well-drained soil. H to 20m (70ft), S 1–6m (3–20ft).

Cyperus papyrus **(Egyptian paper rush)**
Evergreen perennial. Tender, so grow in pots in loam-based compost (John Innes Nos. 2 or 3) in light, dappled or partial shade; stand container in shallow tray of water. Bring indoors in winter. H 2m (6ft), S 0.6m–1.2m (2–4ft).

Ensete ventricosum
'Maurelii'
(Ethiopian banana)
Evergreen perennial. Tender, so grow in pots in loam-based compost (John Innes No. 3) in full sun with shade from hot, midday sun. Bring indoors during winter.
H 6m (20ft), S 5m (15ft).

Ficus carica **(Fig)**
Deciduous tree. Full sun/ partial shade, humus-rich, leafy, moist but well-drained soil. H 3m (10ft), S 4m (12ft).

Geranium x *cantabrigiense*
'Cambridge'
Evergreen perennial. Sunny, well-drained spot.
H 15cm (6in), S 60cm (2ft).

Liriope muscari
(Lilyturf)
Evergreen perennial. Partial or full shade, in light, moderately fertile, preferably acid, moist but well-drained soil.
H 30cm (12in), S 45cm (18in).

Miscanthus sinensis
'Gracillimus'
(Maiden grass)
Deciduous grass. Full sun, moderately fertile, moist but well-drained soil. H 1.3m (4.5ft), S 1.2m (4ft).

Pleioblastus auricomus
Evergreen bamboo. Full sun, fertile, humus-rich, moist but well-drained soil. H and S to 1.5m (5ft).

Polystichum setiferum
Acutilobum Group,
(syn. *P. setiferum*
Proliferum Group)
Evergreen fern. Moist, shady situation, lime-free (acid) soil.
H and S 60–80cm (24–32in).

Spiraea japonica
'Anthony Waterer'
Deciduous shrub. Sun, fertile, moist but well-drained soil.
H and S to 1.5m (5ft).

Zantedeschia aethiopica
'Crowborough'
(Arum lily)
Semi-evergreen perennial. Full sun, humus-rich, moist soil; may need protective mulch in winter.
H 90cm (3ft), S 60cm (2ft).

Above: Tender plants such as clementines and even cannas can be moved into the conservatory for protection during the cold winter months.

This book is published to accompany the television series
Home Front in the Garden, which is produced by the BBC.

Executive producer: Paul Wooding
Series Producer: Patrick Flavelle
Assistant Producer: Julie Richards

Published by BBC Worldwide Ltd, Woodlands,
80 Wood Lane, London W12 0TT

First published 2002

ISBN: 0 563 48857 3
Commissioning Editor: Nicky Copeland
Project Editor: Helena Caldon
Text Editor: Lin Hawthorne
Cover Art Direction: Pene Parker
Book Design: Paul Vater at Sugar Free Design, London
Garden Photography by Robin Mathews
Production Controller: Kenneth McKay

Set in Foundry Sans Light and Caecilia
Printed and bound in Great Britain by
Butler & Tanner Ltd., Frome and London
Colour reproductions by
Radstock Reproductions, Midsomer Norton
Jacket printed by Lawrence-Allen Ltd.,
Weston-super-Mare

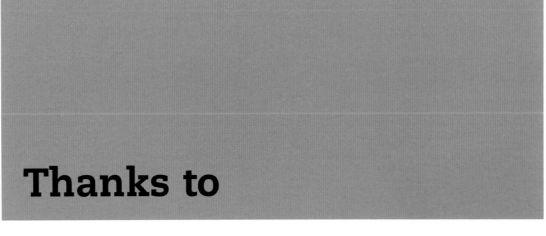

Thanks to

Justine Keane for everything.
Paul Cunningham for his guest appearance.
Sean Cunningham for wonderful commitment and attitude way beyond the call of duty.
Susan Galloway for botanical contributions.
Rachel Innes-Lumsden and Dan Adamson for being the moral guidance in the progression of each series.
Chris Jones for wonderful illustrations and all-round help.
Elma Murray for all the action photographs.
Helena Caldon for seeing the project through and Nicky Copeland and Robin Wood for keeping faith through tough times. Pene Parker, Lin Hawthorne, Paul Vater – thanks it looks great.
Photographer Robin Mathews for his brilliant work as usual.
Sarah, Margi and Andrew at Tendercare.
Jane Root, Nicola Moody, Anne Morrison for still believing and keeping me in work.
Tessa Finch for the move up north.

For all the clients on *Home Front in the Garden* this year – Roy and Patricia, Will and Denise, Jackie and Howard, Sally and Warwick, Mark, Matthew and Kim, Mandy and Hayden.

To the curious Guy and Gordon, Rachel de Thame, Charlie Dimmock.

To the team at John Noel Management – John, Nik, Polly, Debbie, Katherine, Petra, Brian – for trying to keep me from veering off a winding road.

Thanks to Joan, Jack, Declan, Niamh, Emer, Gerry, David, Susan, Terry, Ronan, Jane, Madeleine, Timothy, Karl, Natasha, Julia, Holly, Ben, Rebecca, Jack, Ella, Yayee, Pat, Jane, Eilis, Rory, Niall, Barry Cotter and Sean Keirghan.

Thanks to the Production Team:
Patrick Flavelle – tough but worth it, David Symonds for his brilliant vision, David Smith, Jonathan Barker, Dafydd Palfrey, Julie Richards for the chocolate.

Michelle Davis , Louise Pyne, Jacque Brown, Marilyn Ward, Trudi Cresser, Amanda Crosby, Andrew Painten, Sarah Wilkin, Russell Peers, Simon Harris, Mark Dagwell, Danny Piesley, Russell Minton.

Tom Reed, Strauss Cronje and Ross Britten for being the men on the ground. Matthew Kent, David Eaves, Rob Kershaw, Gerhard Barnard, Stanley Buchanan, James Bowman, Liam Barron, Drew Turner.

Specialist Labour:
Branton Bamford, William Wright, Simon Blau, Eden Palm, Tony Gardner, Richard Hill, Justin and Sam at Basewood Design, Pat Gallagher, Jay Freestone, Jason and Dean Harvey (Factory Furniture), Elite Metalcraft: Tom Gallagher, especially Ryan Tautari for amazing craftsmanship, loyalty and commitment, Grant Thacker and Scott Wilkins.

Rhys, Russ and Cary and all at Virgin Limobikes.
Karen at Jaguar.
John Ferguson – hope to see you back sometime.
Jerry Mecoy, all at OJ Kilkenny, Steve Davies and Paul Martin, Barbara Manton, Jay and Ann.
Tessa Carey, Cynthia Charles, Hannah Weston – for keeping me in check, Paul Midleton and Seb Illis, Fran Price, Lucy Hooper, Trupti Magecha, Josie Milani, Mike Taylor, Paul Woo, Sue Banks, Franny Moyle, Laurence and Jackie Llewelyn-Bowen, Owen Gay and Amanda de Ryk.

suppliers

Decking and Timber

Architectural Reclaim
Theobalds Park Road
Enfield
Middlesex EN2 9BG
Tel: 020 8367 1666
Fax: 020 8367 6668
www.architecturalreclaim.com

Ashwell Recycling
Wick Place Farm
Brentwood Rd
Bulphan
Upminster
Essex RM14 3TL
Tel: 01375 892 576
Fax: 01375 892 330

Country Oak Sussex Ltd
Little Washbrook Farm
Brighton Road
Hurstpierpoint
West Sussex BN6 9EF
Tel: 01273 833869
Fax: 01273 833869

Crestala Fencing
South Farm
Off Brook Lane
Langton Green
Kent TN3 9JN
Tel: 01892 864 646
Fax: 01892 864 366

The Deck Supply Co.
Wyevale Garden Centre
Windmill Lane
Osterley
Middlesex TW7 5PR
Tel: 020 8758 9475
Tel: 020 8347 2124
Email: enquiries@decksupply.co.uk
www.decksupply.co.uk

International Timber
Haven Road
The Hythe
Colchester
Essex CO2 8HU
Tel: 01206 866822
Fax: 01206 878000

Jewson Ltd
Merchant House
Binley Business Park
Binley
Coventry CV3 2TT
Freephone 0800 539766 to find
your nearest branch.

Kilgraney Railway Sleepers
Kilgraney Farm
Owthorpe Road
Cotgrave, Nottingham
Nottinghamshire NG12 3PU
Tel: 07971 914781
Fax: 0115 989 3366
Email: jerrydeacon@bun.com
www.kilgraney.com

Lassco Flooring
Maltby Street
Bermondsey
London SE1 3PA
Tel: 020 7237 4488
Fax: 020 7237 2564
Email: flooring@lassco.co.uk
www.lassco.co.uk

The Loft Shop Ltd
Eldon Way
Littlehampton
BN17 7HE
Tel: 0870 604 0404
Fax: 0870 603 9075
Email: enquiries@loftshop.co.uk
www.loftshop.co.uk

Monks Eleigh Joinery
Paddock Hall
High Street
Monks Eleigh
Ipswich
Suffolk IP7 7AU
Tel: 01449 740 267

Olde English Reclamation
2b Conquest Mill
off Station Road
Ampthill Industrial Estate
Ampthill
Bedfordshire MK45 2QY
Tel: 01525 406 662
Fax: 01525 406 663

The Outdoor Decking Co
Mortimer House
46 Sheen Lane
London SW14 8LP
Tel: 020 8876 8464
Fax: 020 8876 8687
Email: sales@outdoordeck.co.uk
www.outdoordeck.co.uk

Romsey Reclamation
Station Approach
Romsey Railway Station
Romsey, Hants SO51 8DU
Tel: 01794 524 174
Fax: 01794 514 344
www.romseyreclamation.com

S Silverman & Son Importers Ltd
Unit 3 Elstree Distribution Park
Elstree Way
Borehamwood
Herts WD6 1RU
Tel: 020 8327 4000
Fax: 020 8207 0549
Email: info@silverman.co.uk
www.silverman.co.uk

Sleeper Supplies Ltd
PO Box 1377
Kirk Sandall
Doncaster DN3 1XT
Tel: 01302 888 676
Fax: 01302 880 547
Email: sales@sleeper-supplies.co.uk
www.sleeper-supplies.co.uk

A J Smith & Son Ltd
242–4 High Road
Benfleet
Essex SS7 5LA
Tel: 01268 792 771
Fax: 01268 750 780
Email: ajsmith@clara.net
www.ajsmith.clara.net

Timber Decking Association
CIRCE building
Wheldon Road
Castleford
West Yorkshire WF10 2JT
Tel: 01977 712 718
Email: info@tda.org.uk
www.tda.org.uk

Tradelink
25 Beethoven Street
London W10 4LG
Tel: 020 7460 7788
Fax: 020 7460 7799
Email: uk@tradelink-group.com
www.tradelink-group.com

Woodside Timber
56 Spring Lane
London SE25 4SP
Tel: 020 8654 1256
Fax: 020 8655 4010

Woodworking Ltd
Unit 6–7A Kings Yard
Carpenters Rd
Stratford
London E15 2HD
Tel: 020 8986 3332
Fax: 020 8986 3310

Building materials

Altenloh Brinck & Co Ltd
Unit 10 Cedars Business Centre
Avon Road
Cannock
Staffs WS11 1QJ
Tel: 01543 501 910
Fax: 01543 501 919

The Angle Ring Company Ltd
Bloomfield Road
Tipton
West Midlands DY4 9EH
Tel: 0121 557 7241
Fax: 0121 522 4555
www.anglering.co.uk

Arch Coatings UK
A1 Business Park
Knottingley
West Yorkshire WF11 OBH
Tel: 01977 673 363
Fax: 01977 673 521
www.archcoatings.co.uk

Baggeridge Brick
Fir Street
Sedgley, Dudley
West Midlands DY3 4AA
Tel: 01902 880 55
Fax: 01902 880 432
www.baggeridge.co.uk

Camtrak UK Ltd
Unit 6
Highbury Road
Brandon
Suffolk IP27 0ND
Tel: 01842 811 111
Fax: 01842 811 120
Email: camtrakltd@aol.com

C&A Building Plastics
Bidder Street
London E16 4ST
Tel: 020 7474 0474
Fax: 020 7474 5055
Email: info@casupply.co.uk
www.casupply.co.uk

Chiltern Concrete Pumping Services
Loudwater House
London Rd
High Wycombe
Buckinghamshire HP10 9TL
Tel: 01494 472 272
Fax: 01494 441 479

Color 1 Ceramics Limited
404 Richmond Road
Twickenham
Middlesex TW1 2EB
Tel: 020 8891 0691
Fax: 020 8296 0491
Email: info@color1ceramics.com
www.color1ceramics.com

Concrete Developments Ltd
Baltimore Road
Great Barr, Birmingham
Tel: 0800 975 4525
www.concretedevelopments.co.uk

Dorston Reclaimed Materials
The Old Goods Yard
Station Road
Burgess Hill
West Sussex RH15 9DG
Tel: 01444 250 330
Fax: 01444 253 344

Earl Stone Ltd
Sycamore Quarry
Windmill Lane
Kerridge
Macclesfield SK10 5AZ
Tel/Fax: 01625 572 125

E H Smith Ltd
1 Sherborne Road
Acocks Green
Birmingham B27 6AB
Tel: 0121 706 6100

The Gallagher Group
Leitrim House
Coldharbour Lane
Aylesford
Kent ME20 7NS
Tel: 01622 716 543
Fax: 01622 882 366
www.gallagher-group.co.uk

Grundfos Pumps Ltd
Grovebury Road
Leighton Buzzard
Beds LU7 4TL
Tel: 01525 850 000
Fax: 01525 850 011
www.grundfos.com

Harris' Builders Merchants
Charlotte Road
off Maryvale Road
Stirchley, Birmingham
Tel: 0121 451 1664

ISL Renotherm
New Street House
Petworth
West Sussex GU28 0AS
Tel: 01798 343658
Fax: 01798 344 093
www. islrenotherm.co.uk

Johnston Pipes
Doseley, Telford
Shropshire TF4 3BX
Tel: 01952 630 300
Fax: 01952 501 537
www.johnston-pipes.co.uk

Kalon Decorative Products
Huddersfield Road
Birstall, Batley
West Yorkshire WF17 9XA
Tel: 01924 354 000
Fax: 01924 354 001
www.nbsplus.co.uk

Kings Langley Building Supplies
Premier Works, Primrose Hill
Kings Langley
Herts WD4 8HR
Tel: 01923 268 222
Fax: 01923 261 149

Lasershape Ltd
Lilac Grove, Beeston
Notts NG9 1QY
Tel: 0115 925 0269

Lucite International UK Ltd
P O Box 34
Darwen
Lancs BB3 1QB
Tel: 01254 874 000
Fax: 01254 873 300
Email: perspex_online@ineos-a.com.
www.perspex.co.uk

McDermott Bros Contractors Ltd
McDermott House
Cody Road Business Centre
South Crescent
London E16 4TL
Tel: 020 7511 6677
Fax: 020 7511 1114
Email: office@mcdermott-bros.co.uk

McVeigh Parker & Co Ltd
Southend, Bradfield
Nr Reading
Berkshire RG7 6HA
Tel: 0118 974 4777
Fax: 0118 974 4123
Email:
mcveighparker@dial.pipex.com
www.mcveighparker.co.uk

Melcourt Industries Ltd
Boldridge Brake
Long Newnton
Tetbury
Glos GL8 8RT
Tel: 01666 502 711
Fax: 01666 504 398
www.melcourt.co.uk

Monks Eleigh Joinery
Paddock Hall
High Street
Monks Eleigh
Ipswich, Suffolk IP7 7AU
Tel: 01449 740 267

Edmund Nuttall Ltd
Glasgow Road
Kilsith
Glasgow G65 9BL
Tel: 01236 467 050
Fax: 01236 467 072
Email: scotland.office@edmundnuttall.co.uk

Osmose/Protim Solignum Ltd
Fieldhouse Lane
Marlow
Buckinghamshire SL7 1LS
Tel: 01628 484 810
Fax: 01628 481 276
Email: info@osmose.co.uk
www.protimsolignum.com

PL Manufacturing
Cannon Business Park
Unit 14, Gough Road
Bilstone WV14 8XR
Tel: 01902 408 515
Fax: 01902 497 349

RMC Readymix Ltd
RMC House
Rugby
Warwickshire CV21 2DT
Tel 01788 542 111
Fax: 01788 540 166
freephone helpline: 0800 667 827
Email: enquiries.readymix@rmc.co.uk

Sandtex Exterior Paints
Tel: 01254 704 951
www.sandtex.co.uk

Screwfix Direct
Houndslow Business Park
Mead Avenue, Yeovil
Somerset BA22 8BF
Tel: 0500 414 141
www.screwfix.com

Spear and Jackson
Atlas North
Attercliffe
Sheffield S13
Tel: 0114 281 4242
Fax: 0114 281 4252
www.spearandjackson.co.uk

t2 Building Services Ltd
Unit 102, Lea Valley Technopark
Ashley Road
Tottenham N17 9LN
Tel: 020 8880 4600
Fax: 020 8880 4599

Tarmac Southern Limited
Churchward House
Kemble Drive
Swindon SN2 2JA
Tel: 01793 698600

Thermalite
Marley Building Supplies
Station Road
Coleshill
Birmingham BH6 1HP
Tel: 08705 626 500
www.thermalite.co.uk

Welsh Harp Boat Centre
270 West Hendon Broadway
London NW9 6AE
Tel: 020 8202 8677
Email: info@welshharp.co.uk
www.welshharp.co.uk

Xtralite (Rooflights) Ltd
Spencer Road
Blyth Industrial Estate
Blyth
Northumberland
NE24 5TF
Tel: 01670 354 157
Fax: 01670 364 875
www.xtralite.co.uk

Equipment Hire

Bromsgrove Crane Hire
Top Road, Wildmoor
Nr Bromsgrove
Worcs B61 ORD
Tel: 0121 457 7171
Fax: 0121 457 7580
Email: bromsgrove.crane@virgin.net

C & M Skips
28 Spring Hill Passage
Ladywood,
Birmingham B18 7AH
Tel: 0121 454 6255

Cat UK Ltd
Desford
Leicester LE9 9JT
Tel: 01455 826 839
Fax: 01455 826 900
www.cat.com

Danny Collins Supply Co Ltd
54 Swanscombe Street
Swanscombe
Kent DA10 0BN
Tel: 01322 381 111
Fax: 01322 381 706

Elliot Hire
The Fen
Baston, Peterborough
Cambs PE6 9PT
Tel: 01778 560891

H E Services Ltd
Whitewall Road
Strood
Kent ME2 4DZ
Tel: 01634 291 290
Fax: 01634 295 355

Hewden Hire Centre
141 Woolwich Road
Greenwich
London SE10 0RG
Tel: 020 8853 2123
Fax: 020 8853 2310
www.hewden.co.uk

Lynch's
Fourth Way
Wembley
Middlesex HA9 OLH
Tel: 020 8900 0000

Stewart Noel Ltd
Goods Depot
Dickens Street
London SW8 3EP
Tel: 020 7720 7720
Fax: 020 7720 7820

Takeuchi MFG (UK) Ltd
Lynroyle Way
Rochdale
Lancashire OL11 3EX
Tel: 01706 657 722
Fax: 01706 657 744
Email: sales@takeuchi-mfg.co.uk
www.takeuchi-mfg.co.uk

Terranova Lifting Ltd
Terranova House
Bennet Rd, Reading
Berkshire RG2 OQX
Tel: 0118 931 2345
Fax: 0118 931 4114
www.terranova-lifting.co.uk

Glass

Barratts Glass
Unit 64
Merchant Industrial Estate
Verney Road
Bermondsey
London SE16 3DH
Tel: 020 7252 1040
Fax: 020 7252 1080

James Hetley and Co Ltd
Glasshouse Fields
London E1W 3JA
Tel: 020 7780 2344
Fax: 020 7790 2682

Luxcrete
Premier House
Disraeli Road, Park Royal
London NW10 7BT
Tel: 020 8965 7292
Fax: 020 8961 6337
Email: technical@luxcrete.co.uk
www.luxcrete.co.uk

Solaglass
Units 3&4
North Point Business Park
Horton Road
West Drayton
Middlesex UB7 8EQ
Tel: 01895 424 918
Fax: 01895 420 787
www.saint-gobain-glass.com

Wells Glass
1231 Greenford Rd
Sudbury Hill
Greenford
Middlesex UB6 0HY
Tel : 020 8864 6931

Xtralite (Rooflights) Ltd
Spencer Road
Blyth Industrial Estate
Blyth, Northumberland NE24 5TF
Tel: 01670 354 157
Fax:01670 364 875
www.xtralite.co.uk

Lighting

AC/DC Lighting Systems Ltd
Pasture Lane Works
Factory Lane, Barrowford
Lancashire BB9 6ES
Tel: 01282 608 400
Fax: 01282 608 401
Email: sales@acdlighting.net
www.acdclighting.co.uk

Chase Signs Ltd
31/33 Colville Road
South Acton
London W3 8BT
Tel: 020 8992 1153
Fax: 020 8992 4380
www.chase-signs.com

C.R.S Electrical Wholesalers
122 Coombe Lane
London SW20 OBA
Tel: 020 8946 5558
Email:
customerservices@crselectrical.co.uk
www.crselectrical.com

Elliott & Jordan Ltd
(Electrical Contractors)
Unit 51, St Nicholas Road
Littlemore
Oxford OX4 4PN
Tel: 01865 326 221
Fax: 01865 736 680

Evergreen Electrical
3 Invicta Parade
High Street
Sidcup DA14 6ER
Tel/Fax: 020 8309 7722
www.evergreenelectrical.co.uk

Garden and Security Lighting
163g Victoria Road
Horley
Surrey RH6 7AR
Tel: 01293 820 821/822 232
Fax: 01293 824 052
Email: gardenslight@aol.com

Lighting for Gardens Ltd
20 Furmston Court
Icknield Way
Letchworth
Herts SG6 1UJ
Tel: 01462 486 777
Fax: 01462 480 344
Email: sales@lightingforgardens.com
www.lightingforgardens.com

Lighting Technology Projects
2 Tudor Estate
Abbey Road
Park Royal
London NW10 7UY
Tel: 020 8965 6800
Fax: 020 8965 0950
www.lighting-tech.com

Lutron
Lutron House
6 Sovereign Close
Wapping
London E1W 3JF
Tel: 0800 282 107
www.lutron.com

Mr Resistor
21 Lydden Road
London SW18 4LT
Tel: 020 8874 2234
Fax: 020 8871 2262
www.mr-resistor.co.uk

Schott Fibre Optics
Shaw Lane Industrial Estate
Ogden Road
Doncaster DN2 4SQ
Tel: 01302 347 031
Fax: 01302 340 803
www.schott.com/fiberoptics

Wholesale Lighting
34–41 White Lion Street
London N1 9PQ
Tel: 020 7278 8993
Fax: 020 7833 4762

Metalwork

Albert Jagger Ltd
Centaur Works
Green Lane
Walsall
West Midlands WS2 8HG
Tel: 01922 471 000
Fax: 01922 648 021
www.albert-jagger.co.uk

Joseph Ash Galvanizing London
Leven Road
Poplar
London E14 0LP
Tel: 020 7987 5070
Fax: 020 7515 7498

AvestaPolarit
Stevenson Road
Sheffield S9 3XG
Tel: 0114 242 1124
Fax: 0114 242 2152
www.avestapolarit.com

Cannon Steels Ltd
7 Walcot Road
Mill Marsh Lane
Brimsdown
Enfield EN3 7NF
Tel: 020 8805 4070
Fax: 020 8805 4525

Carisbrooke Marine
Unit 1 Lysses Court
High Street
Fareham
Hants PO16 7BE
Tel/Fax: 01329 823 535
Email: carisbrooke@cwcom.net

Creighton & Son Ltd
2 Parr Road
Honeypot Lane
Stanmore
Middlesex HA7 1QA
Tel: 020 8952 8252
Fax: 020 8951 1434
Email: metalman@globalnet.co.uk

Elite Metalcraft Co Ltd
Unit 33, Silicon Business Centre
28 Wadsworth Road
Perivale
Middlesex UB6 7JZ
Tel: 020 8810 5122
Fax: 020 8810 5133
Email: sales@elitemetalcraft.co.uk

Stewart Fraser Ltd
Henwood Industrial Estate
Ashford, Kent TN24 8DR
Tel: 01233 625 911/5
Fax: 01233 633 149
Email: info@stewartfraser.com

Greater London Railing Co
93 Lillie Road
London SW6 7SX
Tel: 020 8876 2256
Fax: 020 8871 4848
Email: glonrailco@aol.com

Integrated Metal Solutions
17b Bakers Court
Paycocke Road, Basildon
Essex SS14 3EH
Tel: 01268 534 133
Fax: 01268 534 134
Email:
info@integratedmetalsolutions.com
www.integratedmetalsolutions.com

Potter & Soar Ltd
Beaumont Rd
Banbury
Oxon OX16 7SD
Tel: 01295 253 344
Fax: 01295 272 132
Email: potter.soar@btinternet.com
www.wiremesh.co.uk

Richardson Roofing Co Ltd
Richardson House
Moor Lane
Staines
Middlesex TW19 6EQ
Tel: 01784 460 044
Email: info@richardson-roofing.com
www.richardson.roofing.co.uk

Sixsmiths Ltd
Gamage Hall Farm
Crowfield Lane
Dymock
Glos GL18 2AE
Tel/Fax: 01531 890 141
Email: sixsmiths@clara.net
www.sixsmiths.clara.net

A J Smith & Son (Benfleet) Ltd
242/4 High Road
Benfleet
Essex SS7 5LA
Tel: 01268 792 771
Fax: 01268 750 780
Email:ajsmith@clara.net
www.ajsmith.clara.net

Sunbeam Metal Works
17/21 Sunbeam Road
Park Royal London NW10 6SP
Tel: 020 8357 1020
Fax: 020 8357 1021
metal@sunbeamgroup.com

Tip Top Trading
Regus Nova Building
Herschel Street
Slough
Berkshire SL1 1XS
Tel: 01753 728 790
Fax: 01753 728 791
www.tiptopalloys.co.uk

suppliers

Misc accessories

Ammira Ltd
Red Brook Mill
Bury Road
Rochdale, Lancashire OL11 4EH
Tel: 01706 356340
Fax: 01706 356 197
Email: salesenquiries@ammira.co.uk
www.ammira.co.uk

Factory Furniture
The Stable Yard
Coleshill
Swindon SN6 7PT
Tel: 01793 763 829
Fax: 01793 861 615
Email: sales@factoryfurniture.co.uk
www.factoryfurniture.co.uk

Hindhead Hot Tubs
Portsmouth Road
Hindhead
Surrey GU26 6AJ
Tel: 01428 605 894
Fax: 01428 609 109
www.hottub.co.uk

Kohler Mira Ltd
Cromwell Road
Cheltenham
Glos GL52 5EP
Tel: 0870 600 0221
Fax: 01242 224 721
Email:
mira_technical@mirashowers.com
www.mirashowers.com

Mexican Hammock Company
42 Beauchamp Road
Bristol BS7 8LQ
Tel/Fax: 0117 942 5353
www.hammocks.co.uk

Modern Garden Company Ltd
Hill Pasture Broxted
Dunmow
Essex CM6 2BZ
Tel/Fax: 01279 851 900
email: info@moderngarden.co.uk
www.moderngarden.co.uk

Nightingale and Son
50 Stuart Road
London SE15 3EB
Tel: 020 7639 4400
Email: sales@nightingaleandsons.co.uk
www.nightingaleandson.co.uk

James Oughtibridge
22 Greenhill Road
Harlesden
London NW10 8UE
Tel: 07880 967 343

The Shed
177 South Croxted Road
West Dulwich
London SE21 8AY
Tel: 020 8488 4418
Email: rreynolds@theshedstudios.com
www.theshedstudios.com

Swan Hattersley Limited
Halesfield 14
Telford, Shropshire TF7 4QR
Tel: 01952 680 288
Fax: 01952 585 629
Email: info@swanhattersley.co.uk
www.swanhattersley.co.uk

twentytwentyone
274 Upper Street
London N1 2UA
Tel/Fax: 020 7288 1996
www.twentytwentyone.com

Robert Welch Studio shop
Lower High Street
Chipping Campden
Glos Gl55 6DY
Tel: 01386 8405 22
Fax: 01386 841 111
www.welch.co.uk

Paint

Crown Paints
Tel: 01254 704951
www.crownpaint.co.uk

Fired Earth Ltd
Twyford Mill
Oxford Road
Adderbury, Banbury
Oxon OX17 3HP
Tel: 01295 812 088
Brochure line: 01295 814 300
Fax: 01295 810 832

W & J Leigh & Co
Tower Works
Kestor Street
Bolton BL2 2AL
Tel: 01204 521 771
Fax: 01204 382 115
Email: enquiries@leighspaints.co.uk
www.wjleigh.co.uk

Edmund Nuttall Ltd
Glasgow Road
Kilsith, Glasgow G65 9BL
Tel: 01236 467 050
Fax: 01236 467 072
Email: scotland.office@edmund-nuttall.co.uk

Sandtex Exterior Paints
Tel: 01254 704 951
www.sandtex.co.uk

Stone, paving, tiling

Albion Stone Quarries
27–33 Brighton Road
Redhill
Surrey RH1 6PP
Tel: 01737 771 772
Fax: 01737 771 776

Alfred McAlpine Slate Ltd
Penrhyn Quarry, Bethesda
Bangor, Gwynedd LL57 4YG
Tel: 01248 600 656
Fax: 01248 601 171
Email: slate@alfred-mcalpine.com
www.amslate.com

Ashby's Plaiting Works
26 Alexandra Road
Ponders End
Enfield EN3 7EH
Tel/Fax: 020 8804 1025

Baggeridge Brick
Fir Street
Sedgley, Dudley
West Midlands DY3 4AA
Tel: 01902 880 555
Fax: 01902 880 432
www.beggeridge.co.uk

Benton Weatherstone Ltd
53 Ferringham Lane
Ferring
West Sussex BN12 5NT
Tel: 01903 243 202
Fax: 01903 503 752

Cavendish Stone Finishes
8 Swinbourne Court
Basildon
Essex SS13 1QA
Tel: 01268 725123
Fax: 01268 728908

Ceramique Internationale
Unit 1, Royds Lane
Leeds LS12 6DU
Tel: 0113 231 0218
Fax: 01113 231 0353
www.ceramiqueinternationale.co.uk

Ceramic Tile Distributors
351 Shields Road
Newcastle upon Tyne NE6 2UD
Tel: 0191 276 1506
www.ctdtiles.co.uk

Comorin Ltd
1 Grieg-y-dderi
Glais
Swansea SA7 9HT
Tel: 01792 844107
Fax: 01792 844 107

Cosmo Ceramics Ltd
515 Lawmoor Street
Dixons Blazes Industrial Estate
Glasgow G5 0TY
Tel: 0141 420 1122
Fax: 0141 429 2838
Email: cosmoceramics@btconnect.com
www.cosmoceramics.co.uk

Cradley Special Brick Co. Ltd.
Congreaves Trading Estate
Cradley Heath
West Midlands B64 7DD
Tel: 01384 635824
Fax: 01384 638266

Dapson Pierce Advertising Ltd
112 High Street
Lower Halling
Kent ME2 1BY
Tel: 01634 244 086
Fax: 01634 241 288
Email: dpaltd@lineone.net

Earl Stone Ltd
Sycamore Quarry
Windmill Lane
Kerridge
Macclesfield
Cheshire SK10 5AZ
Tel/Fax: 01625 572125

Extensive Ltd
Wood End, Prospect Road
Alresford, Hampshire SO24 9QF
Tel: 01962 732 325
Fax: 01962 735 373
Email: info@extensive.co.uk
www.extensive.co.uk

Granit Union
P O Box 5550
Inverness IVI IWD
Tel: 01463 242090
Fax: 01463 242303
Email: info@granitunion.com
www.granitunion.com

Hanson Bath & Portland Stone
Bumpers Lane
Wakeham, Portland
Dorset DT5 1HY
Tel: 01305 820 207
Fax: 01305 860 275
Email: hbps@hanson-aggregates.com

Marshalls
Hall Ings
Southowram
Halifax HX3 9TW
Tel: 01422 306 400
Fax: 01422 306 407
Customer info: 0870 120 7474
Email:
customer.services@marshalls.co.uk
www.marshalls.co.uk

Pinks Hill Landscape Merchants
Off Broad Street
Wood Street Village
Guildford
Surrey GU3 3BP
Tel: 01483 571 620
Fax: 01483 536 816
Email: sales@pinkshill.com
www.pinkshill.com

South Coast Roofing Supplies
Daveys Lane
Lewes
East Sussex BN7 2BQ
Tel: 01273 488 888
Fax: 01273 489 999
Email: info@sigplc.co.uk
www.sigplc.co.uk

Stone Age Ltd
19 Filmer Rd
London SW6 7BU
or 14 King's Rd
Clifton
Bristol BS8 4AB
London tel: 020 7385 7954
Bristol tel: 0117 923 8180
www.estone.co.uk

Stonemarket Ltd
Oxford Road
Ryton-on-Dunsmore
Warwickshire CV8 3EJ
Tel: 02476 518 701
Fax: 02476 518 777

J. Suttle Quarries
California Quarry
Swanage
Dorset BH19 2QS
Tel: 01929 423 576
Fax: 01929 427 656
www.stone.uk.com

Plants

Architectural Plants
Cooks Farm
Nuthurst, Horsham
West Sussex RH13 6LH
Tel: 01403 891772
www.architecturalplants.com

Civic Trees
Forestry House
P O Box 23, Tring
Hertfordshire HP23 4AE
Tel: 01442 825 401
Fax: 01442 890 275
Email: info@civictrees.co.uk
www.civictrees.co.uk

Jungle Giants
Burford House Gardens
Tenbury Wells
Worcestershire WR15 8HQ
Tel: 01584 819 885
email: lynn@junglegiants.co.uk
www.junglegiants.co.uk

The Palm Centre
Ham Central Nursery
Ham Street
Ham, Richmond
Surrey TW10 7HA
Tel: 020 8255 6191
Fax: 020 8255 6192
Email: mail@palmcentre.co.uk
www.palmcentre.co.uk

Pantiles Plant and Garden Centre
Almners Road
Lyne, Chertsey
Surrey KT16 OBJ
Tel: 01932 872195
www.pantiles-nurseries.co.uk

Tendercare
Southlands Road
Denham, Uxbridge
Middlesex UB9 4HD
Tel: 01895 835 544
Fax: 01895 835 036
Email: sales@tendercare.co.uk
www.tendercare.co.uk

Soil

GENERAL SOIL

Atlas Bulk Carriers
The Gravel Pit, Littleton Lane
Shepperton, Middx TW17 ONF
Tel: 01932 569 222
Fax: 01932 569 666

Cottage Farm
Church Road, Milton-under-
Wychwood, Oxon OX7 6LF

Hurleys Turf & Topsoil
Unit 24, Cranborne Road
Industrial Estate,
Potters Bar EN6 3JN
Tel: 0800 026 9981
Fax: 01707 661 060

J Arthur Bowers
Firth Road, Lincoln LM6 7AH
Tel: 01522 537 561
www.william-sinclair.co.uk

Potters Turf and Topsoil
Turpington Lane
Bromley Common
Bromley, Kent BR2 8JN
Tel: 020 8462 4802
Fax: 020 8462 7071

PEAT-FREE GROWING MEDIUM

PBI Home and Garden Ltd
Durkan House
214/224 High Street
Waltham Cross, Herts EN8 7DP
Tel: 01992 784 200
Fax: 01992 784 950
Email: gardening.adviser@pbi.co.uk
www.bio-garden.co.uk

suppliers

Terra Eco-Systems
2nd Floor West
Clearwater Court
Vastern Rd
Reading, Berkshire RG1 8DB
Tel: 0118 373 8784
Fax: 0118 373 8796
Email:
gardening@terraecosystems.com
www.terraecosystems.com

**Thompsons Plant
and Garden Centres**
Perry Street
Chislehurst
Kent BR7 6HA
Tel: 020 8302 2455
Fax: 020 8269 6829

**Wessex Horticultural
Products Ltd**
Wessex House
Units 1–3 Hilltop Business Park
Devizes Road
Salisbury
Wiltshire SP3 4UF
Tel: 01722 337 744
Fax: 01722 333 177
Email: rosemary@wessexhort.co.uk
www.wessexhort.co.uk

Turf

Cumbria Turf
Bank House
Kirkbride
Wigton
Cumbria CA7 5HR
Tel: 01697 351 310
Fax: 01697 351 030
Email: charles.irving@virgin.net

Melcourt Industries Ltd
Boldridge Brake
Long Newnton
Tetbury
Glos GL8 8RT
Tel: 01666 502 711
Fax: 01666 504 398
Email@melcourt.co.uk
www.melcourt.co.uk

Rowlawn (Turf Growers) Ltd
York Road
Elvington
York YO41 4XR
Tel: 01904 608 661
Fax: 01904 608 272
Email: info@rowlawn.co.uk
www.rowlawn.co.uk

Technology

ADT Fire and Security plc
Security House
The Summit
Hanworth Road
Sunbury-on-Thames
Middlesex TW16 5DB
Tel: 01932 743456
Fax: 01932 743222
www.adt.co.uk

Bose Ltd
1 Ambley Green
Gillingham Business Park
Gillingham, Kent ME8 0NJ
Tel: 0870 741 4500
Fax: 0870 741 4545
www.bose.co.uk

Caradon MK Electrical Ltd
The Arnold Centre
Paycocke Road
Basildon
Essex SS14 3EA
Tel: 01268 563 000
Fax: 01268 563 360
www.mkelectric.co.uk

Elliott & Jordan Ltd
(Electrical Contractors)
Unit 51, St Nicholas Road
Littlemore
Oxford OX4 4PN
Tel: 01865 326 221
Fax: 01865 736 680

Glaive Limited
Unit 7, Wren Industrial Estate
Coldred Road
Maidstone
Kent ME15 9YT
Tel/Fax: 01622 664 070
Email: sales@supracables.co.uk
www.supracables.co.uk

KEF Audio UK Ltd
Eccleston Road
Tovil
Maidstone
Kent ME15 6QP
Tel: 01622 672 261
Fax: 01622 750 653
www.kef.com

Link Media Systems Ltd
48/50 St John Street
London EC1M 4DG
Tel: 020 7251 2638 / 2433
Email: info@linkmediasystems.com
www.linkmediasystems.com

NEC
NEC House
1 Victoria Road
Acton, London W3 6BL
Tel: 0845 940 4020
www.nec.co.uk

Owl Video Systems
Horsted Square
Uckfield, East Sussex TN22 1QG
Tel: 01825 766 123
Fax: 01825 760 246
Email:vince@owl-video.co.uk
www.owl-video.co.uk

Pioneer GB Ltd
Pioneer House
Hollybush Hill
Stoke Poges
Slough SL2 4QP
Tel: 01753 789 789
Fax: 01753 789 520
Email: customer_relations
@pgb.pioneer.co.uk
www.pioneer.co.uk

QED Audio Products Ltd
Unit 16, Woking Business Park
Albert Drive
Woking, Surrey GU21 5JY
Tel: 01483 747 474
Fax: 01483 545 600
www.qed.co.uk

**Toshiba/Toshiba Information
Systems UK Ltd**
Toshiba Court
Weybridge Business Park
Addlestone Road
Weybridge, Surrey KT15 2UL
Tel: 01932 841 600
Email: info@toshiba-tiu.co.uk
www.toshiba.co.uk/computers

Veda Custom Install
8 Greyfriars Road
Bury St Edmunds IP32 7DX
Tel: 01284 701101
Email: info@vedacustominstall.co.uk
www.veda-uk.co.uk

Water

David Curtis & Son
Tel: 01322 666 814

Granger Publicity Ltd
New Mills, Slad Road
Stroud
Gloucestershire GL5 1RN
Tel: 01453 750 151
Fax: 01453 759 323
Email: anyone@grangerpublicity.com

Hozelock Ltd
Waterslade House, Thame Road,
Haddenham, Aylesbury,
Buckinghamshire HP17 8JD
Tel: 01844 292 002
Fax: 01844 290 344
www.hozelock.com

South East Galvanizers Ltd
Western Industrial Estate
Witham, Essex CM8 3AW
Tel: 01376 501 501
Fax: 01376 513 410
www.wedge-galv.co.uk

Waterwell Ltd
The Barley Mow Business Centre
Barley New Passage
Chiswick, London W4 4PH
Tel: 020 8742 8855
Email: help@waterwell.co.uk

index

Page numbers in italics refer to illustrations

Abelia x grandiflora 104
Acacia dealbata 112, 116, 146, 174
Acer palmatum 51, *54*, 54, 79, 101
'Burgundy Lace' *102*
Achillea 79, 142
Hoffnung 146, 174
'Lilac Queen' 106
millefolium 'Cerise Queen' *95*, 95
'Moonshine' 81
'Salmon Beauty' 95
Summer Pastels Group 104
achilleas 79
'Moonshine' 81
acid soil 87
Aconitum 104
actinidia 79
Actinidia deliciosa 'Jenny' 50, 54
Actinidia kolomikta 50, 54
Acuba japonica 50
Agave americana 88, 172
'Variegata' *16*, *30*, *88*, 88, 92
agapanthus *92*
Albizia julibrissin 106
alchemillas 102
aloe 88
alstromerias 104
aluminium 60
Anemone 79
x. *hybrida* 'Honorine Joubert' 104
Angelica sylvestris 'Purpurea' 91, *91*
Antarctic beech 112, 116
Aralia elata 81, 106, *125*
Arbutus unedo 98
archways 50
Art Nouveau 106, 125
artemisia 104

Asplenium scolopendrium 91
'Cristatum' 95
Astelia chathamica 88, 92
astilbes 98
astranthias 95
Athyrium niponicum var. *pictum* 95
Aucuba japonica 146, 174
'Crotonifolia' 146
'Rozannie' 146
azaleas 70

bamboos 18, 87, 88, 92, *92*, 96
banana plant 91, 98
baptisias 104
barberry 81
Beardsley, Aubrey 106
beech
Antarctic 112, 116
copper 79, 81
Berberis thunbergii f. 'Atropurpurea' 81, 101
Beschorneria yuccoides 88
Betula
pendula 95, 112, 116, 172
utilis var. *jacquemontii* 98, 101, 172, 174
birches 95, 101, 108, 112, 116
boggy areas 87
Boston ivy 91
Box of Tricks 138–47, 138–46
box plants 76, 81
braziers 44
Brown, Lancelot 'Capability' 11
budgets 23
buildings
concrete walk-through 160, 161
Eyes Wide Shut 48, 48–50, 49
doors on 43, 50
giant egg 74, 76, 77
rolling doors 43
wooden 24, 60

see also dens
Buxus sempervirens 76, 81

Calamagrotsis 98
Californian lifestyle 12
Campanula
glomerata 116
lactiflora 'Loddon Anna' 81
campsis 144, 146
C. x tagliabuana 'Madame Galen' 146
candles 37
cannas 91, 96, 172
C. 'Wyoming' 91, *91*
C. x ehemanii 174
Carex
buchananii 174
comans 88
Carpinus betulus 'Fastigiata' 52, 54, 88, 98
Caryopteris 142
x *clandonensis* 101, 146, 174
case studies
Box of Tricks 138–47, 138–46
Copper Pod 46–55, 46–55
Egghead 72–81, 72–81
Elevation 166–74, 166–74
Meteor 108–17
Catalpa bignoniodes 106, 172
catmint 54, 104
Ceonothus 142, 174
x *delileanus* 'Topaze' 146
Cercis canadensis 91
'Forest Pansy' 104
Cercis siliquastrum 98
Chamerops humilis 88
children 34, 60, 66, 164
and the Egghead garden 75, 75, 76
chimineas 4
chocolate cosmos 91
Choisya ternata 108, 146, 174

Christian cloister gardens 11
Chusan palm 88, 92, 96
Cinescape 162
Citrus reticulata 174
clay soil 87
clematis 79, 81, 104, 174
C. 'Alice Fisk' 81, 116
C. 'Rouge Cardinal' 81
clementines 172, 174
climbing plants 50, 79, 112
clustered bellflower 116
Coastal suburban 164
communal gardens 162, 163
concrete seats 38, 39
conifers, slim-line 88
conservation areas 23
copper beech 79, 81
Copper Pod 46–55, 46–55
Cordyline 93, 98, 106
australis 88
Cornus
controversa 'Variegata' 98
kuosa 98
corrugated metal 60
Cortaderia 98
selloana 88, *88*
Corylus 101
avellana 98, 112, 116
maxima 'Purpurea' 91, 146, 174
Cosmos atrosanguineus 91
Cotinus
coggyyria 101, *101*
'Grace' 96
cottage gardens 104
courtyard gardens 11, 102, 136
crane hire 110
cranesbill 54, 116
Crocosmia
'Lucifer' 88
x. *crocosmiiflora* 88
Crowe, Sylvia 18
Cupressus sempervirens 88, 106, *172*

Curvy 18, 38, 90, 158
Cylindrical 36
Cynara cardunculus 98
Cyperus papyrus 174
Cyrtomium fortunei 95

Dahlia, 'Bishop of Llandaff' 91, *91*
day lilies 81, 104
decking 23, 40, 41, 44, 45, 127
Copper Pod garden 50
Egghead garden 76
roof gardens 130, 130
dens 58–81
Egghead 72–81, 72–81
garden room 68–9, 68
materials 60–70
platforms 70, 70, 71
tower buildings 66, 67
see also pavilions
Dicentra spectabilis 102
Dicksonia
antartica 51, 54, 54, 92, *93*, 96
squarrosa 96
Digitalis
ferruginea 81
grandiflora 116
Divine Proportion 26
Dotty 40, 92
drainage 123
Dryopteris filix-mas 81

Echium piniana 88
Eden Project, Cornwall 96
Egghead 72–81, 72–81
Egyptian gardens 8–11
eighteenth-century gardens 11
Elevation 18, 166–74, 166–74
enclosures 150–74
communal gardens 162, 163
Elevation garden 166–74, 166–74
oval frame 164, 165

index

Ensete ventricosum 'Maurelii'
174
Eryngium 104
Eucalyptus
gunii 98
parviflora 96
Euonymous 79, 95
alatus 96, 101, *101*
fortunei 'Emerald 'n' Gold' 81
japonicus 96, *96*, 146, 174
Euphorbia
characias subsp. *wulfenii* 88
polycroma 88
Eyes Wide Shut 46–55
Exochorda x *macrantha*
'The Bride' 54
exotics 168, 172

Fagus sylvatica Atropurpurea
Group 79, 81
Falling Water 18
Fallopia baldshuanica 112, 116
Fatsia 18
japonica 91, 96, 106
fences 23–4
ferns 79, 87, 91, 95, 98, 101,
112, 116
Festuca glauca 'Elijah Blue'
Ficus carica 174
figs 144
fire pits 43
fireplaces 42, 43
flag iris 92
flooring 65, 127
foam flower 54
foxgloves 81, 112
future of garden design 15–17

gayfeather 116
Geranium 101, 102, 104,
112, 116
himalayense 'Gravetye' 54
macrorrhizum 95, 98
sanguineum 'Max Frei' 81

x *cantabrigiense* 'Cambridge'
174
x *oxonianum* 'Claridge
Druce' 116
Gleditsia triacanthos
'Sunburst' 101, *101*
globeflower, common
European 54
golden hop 54, 79, 112, 117
Golden Mean 26
golden rules of garden
design 24–7
grapes 144
grasses 79, 88, 91, 96, 98, 128
greater woodrush 81
Greek gardens 11
Gunnera 18
manicata 98

ha-has 11
Hart's tongue fern 91, 95
hazels 88, 91, 101, 112, 116, 142
heating 42, 43, 44
Hebe
'Red Edge' 96
vernicosa 146, 174
Hedera 144, 174
canariensis 'Gloire de
Marengo' 146
helix 'Little Diamond' 146
hellebores 18
Hemerocallis *104*, 142
'Pink Damask' 106
'Staghorn Sumach' 54
'Stella de Oro' 81, 104
Heuchera 102
'Palace Purple' 91
cylindrica 'Greenfinch' 102
Hibiscus syriacus
'Oiseau Blue' *66*, 104
High gloss 44, 102, 136
Himalayan birch 101
Himalayan blue poppies 87
history of garden design 8–12

holly, box-leaved 54
honeysuckles 81, 144
hornbeams 52, 54
hostas 79, 91, 102, 106
fortunei 54, *102*, 146, 174
'So Sweet' 54
hot tubs 68
Hovercraft 88, 126
Humulus lupulus 'Aureus' 54,
79, 112, 116
hydrangeas 79, *81*, 106, 125,
142, 174
involucrata 'Hortensis' 146
macrophylla
'Maculata' 146
'Soeur Therese' 81
Hypericum 146, 174

Igloo 96, 160
Ilex 102
crenata 'Golden Gem'
50, *51*, 52, 54, 102
Imperata cyclindrica 'Rubra' 91
Industrial Revolution 11
Iris 79, *92*
pallida 'Variegata' 88, 101
pseudacorus 92
sibirica 'Silver Edge' 81
Islamic gardens 11
Italian cypresses 88
Italian gardens 121
Italian Renaissance gardens 11
ivies 144

Jacobson, Arne 68
Japan 121
Japanese anemones 104
Japanese angelica tree 81
Japanese maples 46, 54, 70,
79, 101, 102
Japanese painted ferns 95
Jencks, Charles 18
Jenga 34, 154
jungle effect 96

Kent, William 11
Kerria japonica 'Pleniflora' 104
Kniphofia caulescens 88

lamb's ears 104
Lavandula
angustifolia 104, *104*, 116,
146, 174
dentata 54, *54*
Lavatera 142
x *clementii* 'Rosea' 104,
146, 174
lavender 102, 116, 142
legal constraints 24–5
levels 121–47
Box of Tricks garden 138–47,
138–46
creating different 128,
128, 129
and drainage 123
Elevation garden 166–75
roof gardens 130, *130*, 131
sloping sites 126, 127,
134, 136, 168
steps 124, *125*, 125, 126,
127, 127
terracing 124, 125, 126,
127, 133
Liatris spicata 91, 96, *96*, 116
lighting 37, 40, 76, 136
Ligularia 18, 79
dentata 95
przewalskii 81
'The Rocket' 54
Linearis polydactyla 81
Liquidamber styraciflua 98, *98*
112, 116
Liriope muscari 174
listed properties 23
Lloyd, Frank 18
Lonicera 81, 144, 146, 174
henryi 81
x *heckrottii* 'Goldflame' 146
low-maintenance gardens 15

lupins 104
Luzula
nivea 81
sylvatica 'Marginata' 81

magnolias 95
Meconopsis 87
medieval monastery gardens 8
metal 17
Meteor 108–17, *108–17*
Miami 62,
mimosa 116
Miscanthus 91, *96*, 98, *98*
sinensis 'Rotsilber' 81
sinensis 'Gracillimus' 174
modern garden design 12–15
monkshood 104
mosaic 44, 136, 137, 158, 168,
172
Musa basjoo 91, *98*

natural laws of proportion 26–7
neighbours, consultation with 24
Nepeta 54, 104
'Six Hills Giant' 54
Nothofagus antarctica 112, 116
Nouveau gardening 106, 124

oasis gardens 8
Olea europaea 92
olive trees 92
Ophiopogon planiscapus
'Nigrescens' 91, 101
Osmanthus heterophyllus 102
Osmunda regalis
'Purpurascens' 116
Oxalis triangularis
'Atropurpurea' 91

Paeonia lactiflora
'Karl Rosenfield' 81
'Sarah Bernhardt' 54
palms 87, 88, 96
Papaver

index

orientale 104
somniferum 91, 104
Parthenocissus
    henryana 81
    tricuspidata 'Veitchii' 91
parties 37
passionflower (*Passiflora*)
    144, 146, 174
    P. 'Amethyst' 146
patios 168
pavilions
    Box of Tricks 140
    Miami beach 62, 62, 63
    Moroccan hideaway 64, 65, 65
peach, ornamental 98
pearl bush 54
pennisetum setaceum 98
peonies 104
Persicaria bistorta 'Superba' 81
Phormium 84, 93, 98
    tenax 91
Phyllostachys
    aurea 88
    nigra 88, 91
Physocarpus opulifolius 146, 174
    'Dart's Gold' 146
Pieris 46
Pinus mugo 102, 174
Pittosporum tobira 88, 174
Pleioblastus auricomus 174
Poles apart 70, 134
Polygonatum humile 54
Polypodium vulgare 116
Polystichum setiferum 95, 116
ponds 48, 101, 128
poppies 87, 91, 104
potentillas 101, 142, 146, 174
    P. fructicosa 'Goldfinger' 146
    P. fructicosa 'Jackman's
        Variety' 146
Principle of Thirds 26
proportion, natural laws of 26
Prunus persica 'Nana' 98
Pseudopanax ferox 88

railway sleepers 60, 127, 155
raised beds 44, 102, 133, 136
Ramped 94, 128
Rapunzel 66, 104
red-hot pokers 88
Repton, Humphrey 98
Rheum palmatum 102
Rhus typhina 'Dissecta' 101
Robinia pseudoacacia 'Frisia'
    108, 112
Roman gardens 11
roof gardens 130, 130, 131
'room outdoors' concept 12, 32
rosemary (*Rosmarinus*
    officinalis) 18, 81, 104, *104*,
    106
roses (*Rosa*) 79, 104, 112
    Agatha Christie 104
    Eglantyne 104
    High Hopes 104
    rugosa 'Alba' 54, 146, 174
    'Wiltshire' 116
royal fern 116
Royal Horticultural Society,
    Plant Finder 87
rusty foxglove 81

Salix
    alba subsp. *vitellina* 88, *88*
    babylonica var. *pekinensis*
        98
Salvia officinalis 98, 106,
    146, 174
Sambucus nigra 'Gerda' 91
sandy soil 87
Santolina
    chamaecyparissus 98
    rosmarinifolia 54
Sasa veitchii 88
sea hollies 98
seaside gardens 104, 164
seating 38, 39, 153
    egg chair 68, 69
    fixed seating 39

hanging seats 110
Meteor garden 110–11,
    111, 113
    for parties 37
    swinging chairs 37
Sedum 96, 101
    herbstefreude 81
    spectabile 95
shady areas 87
sheds 24
shower rooms 34, 35, 155
shrubs 87
silver birch 95, 112, 116
Sisyrinchium striatum 88
skimmia 79
sloping sites 126, 127, 134, 136
smoke bush 96
snowy woodrush 81
soft shield fern 95, 116
Solanum crispum
    'Glasnevin' 144, 146, 174
Solidago 95
Sorbus 95
    aria 101
Spiraea
    japonica 54, 116
        'Anthony Waterer' 174
        'Crispa' 54
        'Little Princess' 116
    x vanhouttei 54
Stachys byzantina 95, 104
star jasmine 116
steps *124*, 125, 125, 126, *127*, 127
Stilted 43, 64
Stipa 89, 91
    gigantea 88
strawberry tree 98
surveillance systems 75
sweet gum 112, 116
swimming pools 156, 156, 157
Tasmanian tree fern 54
Taxus baccata 'Fastigiata' 88
telegraph poles 60, 65, 70,
    134, 135

television screens 32
terracing 11, 124, 125, 126,
    127, 133
Thuja 98
    occidentallis 'Smaragd' 88
thyme (*Thymus*) 79, 116
    'Doone Valley' 116
    vulgaris 'Silver Posie' 116
Tiarella cordifolia 54
To the waters and wild 100
Torpedo 68, 132
tower buildings 66, 67
Trad Mod 98, 156
Trachelospermum jasminoides
    116
Trachycarpus fortunei 85, 88, 92,
    96
tree ferns 128
trees 87, 100
Trollius europaeus 54
Tulbaghia violacea 104, *106*

Uncinia rubra 81
Upstairs downstairs 130

Verbena bonariensis 106
Viburnum
    davidii 88, 91, 146, 174
    opulus 'Roseum' 81
Vinca minor 'Atropurpurea'
    146, 174
violas 91, 104
Virginia creeper 81

walled gardens 151
walls 23–4, 136, 137, 168
water
    ponds 48, 101, 128
    roof gardens 130
    showers 34, 35
western red cedar 60, 74, 158
whitebeam 101
winged spindle 96, 101
wooden buildings 24, 60

wooden enclosures 152, 158,
    159
wooden flooring 65, 127
wooden platforms 70, 70, 71

Xanthorrhoea australis 91

yarrow 81
yuccas 88

Zantedeschia 98, 172
    aethiopica 'Crowborough'
        174